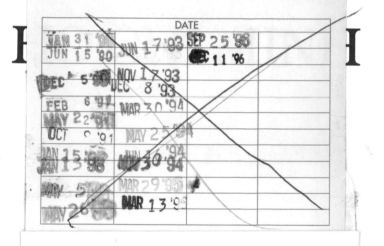

DATE			
JAN 31 '9	JUN 17 '93	SEP 25 '95	
JUN 15 '90		EC 11 '96	
DEC 5 '9	NOV 17 '93		
	DEC 8 '93		
FEB 6 '9	MAR 30 '94		
MAY 22 '9			
OCT 9 '91	MAY 25 '94		
JAN 15 '9	MAY 30 '94		
MAY 5	MAR 29 '95		
MAY 26	MAR 13 '9		

JUN 16 '88

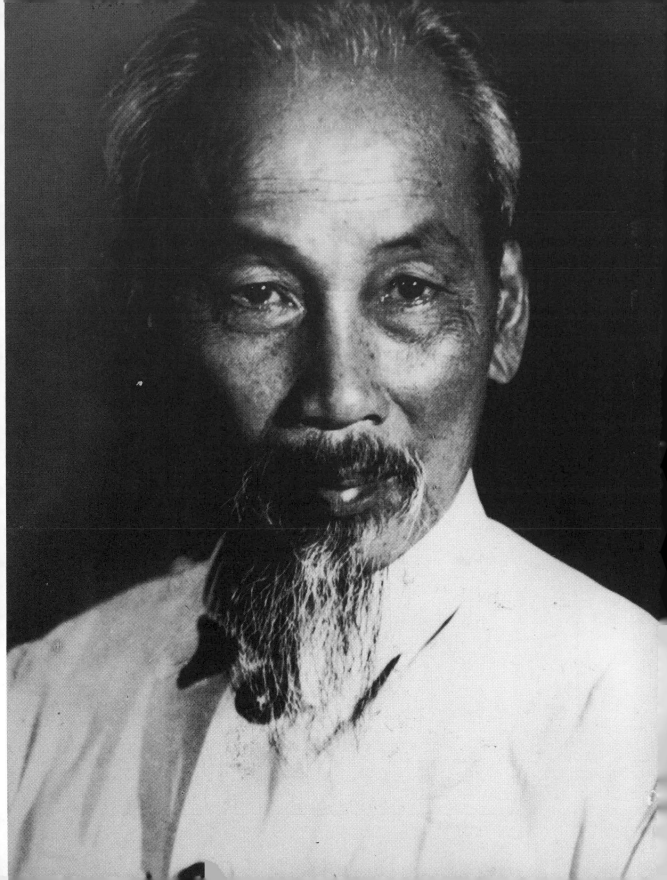

HO CHI MINH

Dana Ohlmeyer Lloyd

1986
CHELSEA HOUSE PUBLISHERS
NEW YORK
NEW HAVEN   PHILADELPHIA

SENIOR EDITOR: William P. Hansen
PROJECT EDITOR: John W. Selfridge
EDITORIAL COORDINATOR: Karyn Gullen Browne
ASSISTANT EDITOR: Bert Yaeger
EDITORIAL STAFF: Maria Behan
　　　　　　　Susan Friedman
　　　　　　　Perry Scott King
　　　　　　　Kathleen McDermott
　　　　　　　Howard Ratner
　　　　　　　Alma Rodriguez-Sokol
ART DIRECTOR: Susan Lusk
LAYOUT: Irene Friedman
ART ASSISTANTS: Noreen Lamb
　　　　　　　Carol McDougall
　　　　　　　Victoria Tomaselli
COVER ILLUSTRATION: Don Longabucco
PICTURE RESEARCH: Karen Herman

Frontispiece courtesy of Eastfoto.

First Printing

Library of Congress Cataloging in Publication Data

Lloyd, Dana Ohlmeyer. HO CHI MINH.

(World leaders past & present)
Bibliography: p.
Includes index.
　1. Ho Chi Minh, 1890–1969. 2. Vietnam (Democratic
Republic)— Presidents—Biography I. Title. II. Series
DS560.72.H6L57　　1986　　959.704′092′4　[B] [92]　86-13707

ISBN 0-87754-571-5

Chelsea House Publishers

133 Christopher Street, New York, NY 10014

345 Whitney Avenue, New Haven, CT 06510

5014 West Chester Pike, Edgemont, PA 19028

Contents

ADENAUER
ALEXANDER THE GREAT
MARC ANTONY
KING ARTHUR
ATATÜRK
ATTLEE
BEGIN
BEN-GURION
BISMARCK
LÉON BLUM
BOLÍVAR
CESARE BORGIA
BRANDT
BREZHNEV
CAESAR
CALVIN
CASTRO
CATHERINE THE GREAT
CHARLEMAGNE
CHIANG KAI-SHEK
CHURCHILL
CLEMENCEAU
CLEOPATRA
CORTÉS
CROMWELL
DANTON
DE GAULLE
DE VALERA
DISRAELI
EISENHOWER
ELEANOR OF AQUITAINE
QUEEN ELIZABETH I
FERDINAND AND ISABELLA
FRANCO

FREDERICK THE GREAT
INDIRA GANDHI
MOHANDAS GANDHI
GARIBALDI
GENGHIS KHAN
GLADSTONE
GORBACHEV
HAMMARSKJÖLD
HENRY VIII
HENRY OF NAVARRE
HINDENBURG
HITLER
HO CHI MINH
HUSSEIN
IVAN THE TERRIBLE
ANDREW JACKSON
JEFFERSON
JOAN OF ARC
POPE JOHN XXIII
LYNDON JOHNSON
JUÁREZ
JOHN F. KENNEDY
KENYATTA
KHOMEINI
KHRUSHCHEV
MARTIN LUTHER KING, JR.
KISSINGER
LENIN
LINCOLN
LLOYD GEORGE
LOUIS XIV
LUTHER
JUDAS MACCABEUS
MAO ZEDONG

MARY, QUEEN OF SCOTS
GOLDA MEIR
METTERNICH
MUSSOLINI
NAPOLEON
NASSER
NEHRU
NERO
NICHOLAS II
NIXON
NKRUMAH
PERICLES
PERÓN
QADDAFI
ROBESPIERRE
ELEANOR ROOSEVELT
FRANKLIN D. ROOSEVELT
THEODORE ROOSEVELT
SADAT
STALIN
SUN YAT-SEN
TAMERLANE
THATCHER
TITO
TROTSKY
TRUDEAU
TRUMAN
VICTORIA
WASHINGTON
WEIZMANN
WOODROW WILSON
XERXES
ZHOU ENLAI

───── ON LEADERSHIP ─────
Arthur M. Schlesinger, jr.

LEADERSHIP, it may be said, is really what makes the world go round. Love no doubt smooths the passage; but love is a private transaction between consenting adults. Leadership is a public transaction with history. The idea of leadership affirms the capacity of individuals to move, inspire, and mobilize masses of people so that they act together in pursuit of an end. Sometimes leadership serves good purposes, sometimes bad; but whether the end is benign or evil, great leaders are those men and women who leave their personal stamp on history.

Now, the very concept of leadership implies the proposition that individuals can make a difference. This proposition has never been universally accepted. From classical times to the present day, eminent thinkers have regarded individuals as no more than the agents and pawns of larger forces, whether the gods and goddesses of the ancient world or, in the modern era, race, class, nation, the dialectic, the will of the people, the spirit of the times, history itself. Against such forces, the individual dwindles into insignificance.

So contends the thesis of historical determinism. Tolstoy's great novel *War and Peace* offers a famous statement of the case. Why, Tolstoy asked, did millions of men in the Napoleonic wars, denying their human feelings and their common sense, move back and forth across Europe slaughtering their fellows? "The war," Tolstoy answered, "was bound to happen simply because it was bound to happen." All prior history predetermined it. As for leaders, they, Tolstoy said, "are but the labels that serve to give a name to an end and, like labels, they have the least possible connection with the event." The greater the leader, "the more conspicuous the inevitability and the predestination of every act he commits." The leader, said Tolstoy, is "the slave of history."

Determinism takes many forms. Marxism is the determinism of class. Nazism the determinism of race. But the idea of men and women as the slaves of history runs athwart the deepest human instincts. Rigid determinism abolishes the idea of human freedom—

the assumption of free choice that underlies every move we make, every word we speak, every thought we think. It abolishes the idea of human responsibility, since it is manifestly unfair to reward or punish people for actions that are by definition beyond their control. No one can live consistently by any deterministic creed. The Marxist states prove this themselves by their extreme susceptibility to the cult of leadership.

More than that, history refutes the idea that individuals make no difference. In December 1931 a British politician crossing Park Avenue in New York City between 76th and 77th Streets around 10:30 P.M. looked in the wrong direction and was knocked down by an automobile—a moment, he later recalled, of a man aghast, a world aglare: "I do not understand why I was not broken like an eggshell or squashed like a gooseberry." Fourteen months later an American politician, sitting in an open car in Miami, Florida, was fired on by an assassin; the man beside him was hit. Those who believe that individuals make no difference to history might well ponder whether the next two decades would have been the same had Mario Constasino's car killed Winston Churchill in 1931 and Giuseppe Zangara's bullet killed Franklin Roosevelt in 1933. Suppose, in addition, that Adolf Hitler had been killed in the street fighting during the Munich *Putsch* of 1923 and that Lenin had died of typhus during World War I. What would the 20th century be like now?

For better or for worse, individuals do make a difference. "The notion that a people can run itself and its affairs anonymously," wrote the philosopher William James, "is now well known to be the silliest of absurdities. Mankind does nothing save through initiatives on the part of inventors, great or small, and imitation by the rest of us—these are the sole factors in human progress. Individuals of genius show the way, and set the patterns, which common people then adopt and follow."

Leadership, James suggests, means leadership in thought as well as in action. In the long run, leaders in thought may well make the greater difference to the world. But, as Woodrow Wilson once said, "Those only are leaders of men, in the general eye, who lead in action. . . . It is at their hands that new thought gets its translation into the crude language of deeds." Leaders in thought often invent in solitude and obscurity, leaving to later generations the tasks of imitation. Leaders in action—the leaders portrayed in this series—have to be effective in their own time.

And they cannot be effective by themselves. They must act in response to the rhythms of their age. Their genius must be adapted, in a phrase of William James's, "to the receptivities of the moment." Leaders are useless without followers. "There goes the mob," said the French politician hearing a clamor in the streets. "I am their leader. I must follow them." Great leaders turn the inchoate emotions of the mob to purposes of their own. They seize on the opportunities of their time, the hopes, fears, frustrations, crises, potentialities. They succeed when events have prepared the way for them, when the community is awaiting to be aroused, when they can provide the clarifying and organizing ideas. Leadership ignites the circuit between the individual and the mass and thereby alters history.

It may alter history for better or for worse. Leaders have been responsible for the most extravagant follies and most monstrous crimes that have beset suffering humanity. They have also been vital in such gains as humanity has made in individual freedom, religious and racial tolerance, social justice and respect for human rights.

There is no sure way to tell in advance who is going to lead for good and who for evil. But a glance at the gallery of men and women in *World Leaders—Past and Present* suggests some useful tests.

One test is this: do leaders lead by force or by persuasion? By command or by consent? Through most of history leadership was exercised by the divine right of authority. The duty of followers was to defer and to obey. "Theirs not to reason why,/ Theirs but to do and die." On occasion, as with the so-called "enlightened despots" of the 18th century in Europe, absolutist leadership was animated by humane purposes. More often, absolutism nourished the passion for domination, land, gold and conquest and resulted in tyranny.

The great revolution of modern times has been the revolution of equality. The idea that all people should be equal in their legal condition has undermined the old structure of authority, hierarchy and deference. The revolution of equality has had two contrary effects on the nature of leadership. For equality, as Alexis de Tocqueville pointed out in his great study *Democracy in America*, might mean equality in servitude as well as equality in freedom.

"I know of only two methods of establishing equality in the political world," Tocqueville wrote. "Rights must be given to every citizen, or none at all to anyone . . . save one, who is the master of all." There was no middle ground "between the sovereignty of all and the absolute power of one man." In his astonishing prediction of 20th-century totalitarian dictatorship, Tocqueville explained how the revolution of equality could lead to the *"Führerprinzip"* and more terrible absolutism than the world had ever known.

But when rights are given to every citizen and the sovereignty of all is established, the problem of leadership takes a new form, becomes more exacting than ever before. It is easy to issue commands and enforce them by the rope and the stake, the concentration camp and the *gulag.* It is much harder to use argument and achievement to overcome opposition and win consent. The Founding Fathers of the United States understood the difficulty. They believed that history had given them the opportunity to decide, as Alexander Hamilton wrote in the first Federalist Paper, whether men are indeed capable of basing government on "reflection and choice, or whether they are forever destined to depend . . . on accident and force."

Government by reflection and choice called for a new style of leadership and a new quality of followership. It required leaders to be responsive to popular concerns, and it required followers to be active and informed participants in the process. Democracy does not eliminate emotion from politics; sometimes it fosters demagoguery; but it is confident that, as the greatest of democratic leaders put it, you cannot fool all of the people all of the time. It measures leadership by results and retires those who overreach or falter or fail.

It is true that in the long run despots are measured by results too. But they can postpone the day of judgment, sometimes indefinitely, and in the meantime they can do infinite harm. It is also true that democracy is no guarantee of virtue and intelligence in government, for the voice of the people is not necessarily the voice of God. But democracy, by assuring the right of opposition, offers built-in resistance to the evils inherent in absolutism. As the theologian Reinhold Niebuhr summed it up, "Man's capacity for justice makes democracy possible, but man's inclination to injustice makes democracy necessary."

A second test for leadership is the end for which power is sought. When leaders have as their goal the supremacy of a master race or the promotion of totalitarian revolution or the acquisition and exploitation of colonies or the protection of greed and privilege or the preservation of personal power, it is likely that their leadership will do little to advance the cause of humanity. When their goal is the abolition of slavery, the liberation of women, the enlargement of opportunity for the poor and powerless, the extension of equal rights to racial minorities, the defense of the freedoms of expression and opposition, it is likely that their leadership will increase the sum of human liberty and welfare.

Leaders have done great harm to the world. They have also conferred great benefits. You will find both sorts in this series. Even "good" leaders must be regarded with a certain wariness. Leaders are not demigods; they put on their trousers one leg after another just like ordinary mortals. No leader is infallible, and every leader needs to be reminded of this at regular intervals. Irreverence irritates leaders but is their salvation. Unquestioning submission corrupts leaders and demands followers. Making a cult of a leader is always a mistake. Fortunately hero worship generates its own antidote. "Every hero," said Emerson, "becomes a bore at last."

The signal benefit the great leaders confer is to embolden the rest of us to live according to our own best selves, to be active, insistent, and resolute in affirming our own sense of things. For great leaders attest to the reality of human freedom against the supposed inevitabilities of history. And they attest to the wisdom and power that may lie within the most unlikely of us, which is why Abraham Lincoln remains the supreme example of great leadership. A great leader, said Emerson, exhibits new possibilities to all humanity. "We feed on genius. . . . Great men exist that there may be greater men."

Great leaders, in short, justify themselves by emancipating and empowering their followers. So humanity struggles to master its destiny, remembering with Alexis de Tocqueville: "It is true that around every man a fatal circle is traced beyond which he cannot pass; but within the wide verge of that circle he is powerful and free; as it is with man, so with communities."

—*New York*

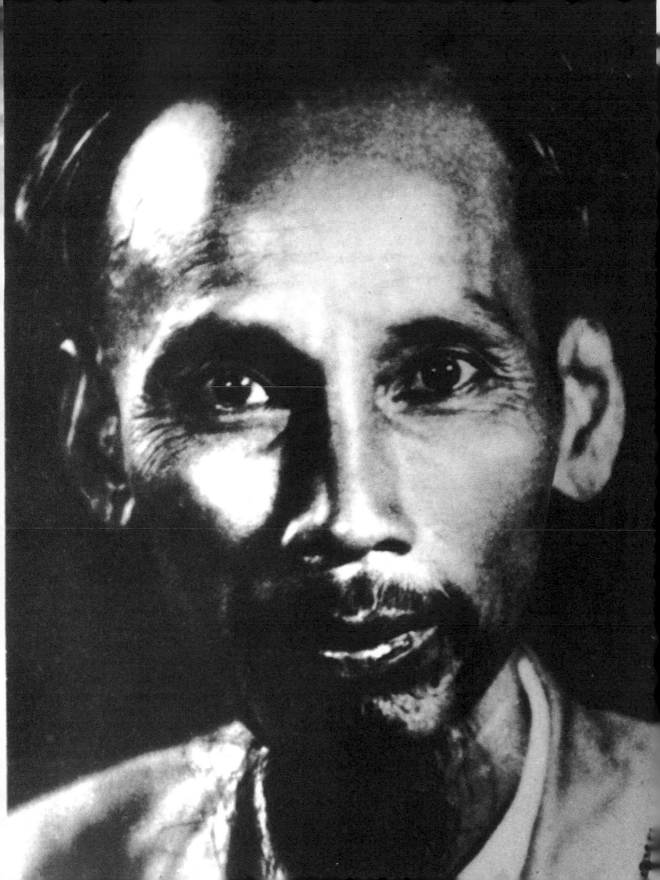

1

The Child of Rebellion

On a bleak winter's day in Paris, 1919, a thin, clean-shaven young man boarded a train for Versailles. Ho Chi Minh was eager to attend the peace conference being held there. It marked the end of World War I and a new beginning for many of the countries of the world. Nestled in the pocket of his rented black woolen suit was a list of suggestions he hoped would change the future of his homeland — the small Asian nation of Vietnam.

Ho was anxious to negotiate with the Western leaders at the conference for specific freedoms for Vietnam, a nation under the crushing heel of French colonialism for more than half a century. The idealistic 29-year-old hoped that he would find at least one sympathizer at the conference — the United States President Woodrow Wilson.

The American leader had stated that the victorious Allies had been fighting for the self-determination of all peoples. In fact, it was Wilson's words that had motivated Ho to put together his list of suggestions, which included ideas drawn directly from the American Bill of Rights.

Ho had been greatly encouraged by President Wilson's "14 Points," a plan, announced in January 1917, for a fair settlement after the Central Powers

The Vietnamese communist revolutionary leader Ho Chi Minh as he appeared in the early 1950s. Ho dedicated himself in 1919 to winning Vietnam's independence and unification. His Vietminh nationalist movement eventually ousted French occupiers in 1954.

UPI/BETTMANN NEWSPHOTOS

A Southeast Asian peasant carrying a European missionary across a stream in the early 1900s. Since the mid-1800s, France had begun imposing its military and governmental presence, Christianity, and the Western (Latin) alphabet upon the Vietnamese people. Anti-French uprisings in reaction to this imposition influenced Ho as a child.

(Germany, Turkey, and Austria-Hungary) were eventually defeated. In these 14 Points, Wilson asked that free navigation of the seas be guaranteed; that occupied territories such as Belgium, Romania, and Serbia (now part of Yugoslavia), be evacuated; and that national groups under Turkish domination be granted the right to self-government. Under Wilson's plan, Poland would be given its independence, and even Austria-Hungary would be permitted to govern itself after its defeat. For the young Vietnamese patriot, probably the most important of these points was that the native populations of colonies should not be ignored. Rather than heeding only the interests of nations that held claims to colonies, the interests of these colonies' populations would be given equal consideration.

As the day wore on, the young man's hopes began to fade. Night soon came and he never saw the president. As he walked away from the palace, Ho realized that the wealthy, more powerful nations would never easily surrender their colonies. The Vietnamese, like the rest of the oppressed peoples whose nations were not yet their own, would ultimately have to fight for their freedom.

Back on the train to Paris, Ho tucked his suggestions into his coat pocket and smiled, remembering he had to return the suit to the rental store the next morning. Days later, the letter he had sent to Wilson returned unopened. As time passed, he became more determined, and more resilient, always sticking by his pledge to spend the rest of his life fighting for the freedom of his people. Calm and simple, this frail young man would soon become a political tiger that would claw at the backs of the powerful nations until they finally were forced to reckon with him.

Ho Chi Minh was born on May 19, 1890, as Nguyen Sinh Cung. Throughout his life, Ho would often change his name, using aliases as decoys for the French, British, and Chinese police who followed him in confusion until the day he became the national leader of Vietnam. Though he assumed the alias Ho Chi Minh relatively late in his life, it remains his most familiar name.

> *The Vietnam into which Ho was born in 1890 was a bitter land; the French ruled, but they ruled by force alone.*
> —DAVID HALBERSTAM
> American journalist and historian

14

Like most Vietnamese provinces, Nghe An, the province of Ho's birth, had poor farming conditions and was overcrowded with destitute peasants. These conditions created restlessness and unruly discontent among the people. Nghe An is often considered to have been the cradle of Vietnamese nationalism. When France had gained colonial control over most of Vietnam, Phan Dinh Phung, a member of the class of scholarly officials called mandarins,

The Great Court of the palace at Versailles near Paris, France. Ho Chi Minh came here in 1919, during the peace conference following World War I, with an Eight Point proposal aimed at gaining independence for the Vietnamese people, but was refused entry into the conference.

began the "Scholars' Revolt" that went on from 1885 to 1895.

The French had arrived in Vietnam as early as the 17th century. One mission in particular, led by a Jesuit priest named Alexandre de Rhodes, converted tens of thousands of Vietnamese to Catholicism. Though the French mission was eventually discontinued, subsequent generations of Catholic Vietnamese were persecuted and were forced to fight internal wars for their own survival. The French returned during the 1850s to defend the Catholic Vietnamese, and established Indochina as a colony. The area consisted of five regions — Cambodia, Laos, and three Vietnamese provinces. Tonkin lay in the north, with its capital at Hanoi; in southern Vietnam was Cochin China, whose capital was Saigon; between them was Annam (Ho's homeland), with its capital at Hué. The Vietnamese emperor, whose dynasty had ruled a united country for one and a half centuries, was given little power by the French.

French capitalists soon invested fortunes in rubber plantations and large agricultural holdings. This contradicted the Vietnamese concept of land. The Vietnamese villagers believed that working for money was evil. The Vietnamese family held a small parcel of land from which they provided for their needs, and all families contributed to the livelihood of their village. Theirs was a society based on sharing and cooperation — not on the competitive pursuit of money.

The French expected the Vietnamese quickly to embrace modern concepts. The colonialists lacked an understanding of the simplicity and beauty of the very old cultural traditions of the area, while the Vietnamese were not willing to give up their own nationality and to accept the culture of the French. It was this cultural pride that fueled the anger in men such as Ho's father Nguyen Sinh Huy.

During Ho's early youth in the village of Kim Lien, his father tended the family water buffalo by day and studied by night. Nguyen Sinh Huy passed the civil service exam when Ho was eight years old and moved the family to Hué, the capital of the Annam

Our rivers and our mountains have been annexed by [the French] at a stroke and turned into a foreign territory.
—PHAN DINH PHUNG
19th-century nationalist rebel

province. Here young Ho learned of the dramatic differences in the way the French and the Vietnamese lived.

Two years after their arrival in Hué, Ho's father left on a 250-mile journey to take the next set of civil service exams. The trip along Vietnam's limited road system would be long and hard. Nguyen Sinh Huy would have to travel mainly by foot on high and treacherous mountain trails. While he was away tragedy struck at home.

Ho's mother died during childbirth. Nguyen Sinh Huy would not be able to return for many weeks,

From left to right: French Premier Georges Clemenceau, United States President Woodrow Wilson, Baron Giorgio Sonnino of Italy (back turned), and British Prime Minister David Lloyd George, after signing the Treaty of Versailles, which set peace terms for World War I. Ho believed President Wilson would be sympathetic to his plan for Vietnamese independence.

17

La Liberté Conduisant le Peuple (Liberty Leading the People) by the preeminent French Romantic painter Eugène Delacroix. Personifying the struggle for freedom, a woman carries a rifle and the French flag in this painting inspired by the 1848 Paris revolution. French revolutionary thinkers greatly influenced Ho.

and the children were left alone to grieve and care for themselves. Ten-year-old Ho was thus forced prematurely into adulthood.

To the French colonists it seemed that the days of resistance were over, and that by 1900 the French way of doing things had triumphed. One colonist asserted: "Administratively, Vietnamese patriotism was dead, and those who rose against us were 'outlaws.'"

Many of Ho's ancestors had been intellectuals, small landowners, and administrators. His grandfather had even held a somewhat high position as a district governor under the French, but was removed due to his disobedience toward the colonial government. Shortly after passing his exams, Ho's father refused to accept appointments to the civil service, but instead supported his family by teaching. Finally, bowing to official and village pressure, he reluctantly accepted an administrative post in the Ministry of Rites. His political opinions did not allow him to remain there long, however. Nguyen Sinh Huy joined the *Dong Kinh Nghia Thuc*, the Private Schools' (or Scholars') movement in 1907. The movement had been named after a major school based in Hanoi, the largest city in French-controlled Tonkin in northern Vietnam. This organization stood for the idea that the Vietnamese scholarly class could bring Vietnam into the modern age, and enable the country to participate in commerce and industry. Between 1907 and 1908 nationalism flared up, and plots were devised to overthrow the foreign intruders. The French were angered and responded violently.

Before the French firmly established French Indochina in 1884, most Vietnamese were literate. They wrote in Chinese symbols, or *Chu Han*, called ideograms. When the French made Vietnam a colony and divided the country into three regions, they imposed a new official Vietnamese language. Instead of the Chinese symbols, all writing had to be done using the Western (Latin) alphabet. The new alphabet came to be known as *quoc-ngu*. This change never reached the villages, so most of the peasants were unable to read or write the new official Vietnamese language. This created a rift between social classes.

The anti-French attitude of Nguyen Sinh Huy affected not only Ho, but also his brother and sister. Ho and his older brother, Khiem, were errand boys and message carriers for the revolutionaries before they were nine years old. Their sister, Thanh, became a gunrunner for the rebels and spent time in jail for her actions. She became engaged to a young revolutionary who perished on the island prison Con-lon, or Poulo Condore, as it was called by the French. Devotion to the anticolonial movement made it difficult for the Nguyen family to stay together, and its members soon went separate ways.

When I was young I studied Buddhism, Confucianism, Christianity, as well as Marxism. There is something good in each doctrine.
—HO CHI MINH

Nguyen Sinh Huy introduced his youngest son to many of his revolutionary friends; the most famous, and the one Ho would see several times in the future, was the poet and patriot Phan Boi Chau.

Throughout Ho's childhood there were many uprisings in Vietnam, as groups of rebels fought to free their country from the French. Phan Boi Chau had organized an uprising on July 14, 1901, during the French celebration of their own independence, known as Bastille Day. As with many uprisings at the time, this one was a failure because the French found out about it in advance and squelched it. Eleven years old at the time, Ho would come to realize that if a rebellion was to be successful, it had to be kept a secret from the French.

Phan had fled Vietnam and French rule in 1901 for Japan. There he wrote a protest article that caused a sensation in Vietnam and influenced Ho in his later days as a journalist. Phan argued that traditional ideas could be used to support uprisings against foreign occupiers. In his articles, Phan referred to Mencius, an ancient Chinese philosopher, highly regarded among the Vietnamese — especially educated officials. Mencius, who taught during the 4th century B.C., stated that, once in office, a ruler must "practice his principles for the good of the people . . . [and] be above the power of worldly riches and honors. . . ."

Young Ho received a solid education because of his father's position in government. When he was 13, his father enrolled him in a private school run by the French. These Franco-Annamite schools were intended to rid the Vietnamese of their national identity. But there was even information of French origin that the colonial schools found it necessary to suppress: the democratic ideas of France's great 18th-century thinkers, Jean-Jacques Rousseau, Montesquieu, and Voltaire. Although Ho was a talented student, his rebellious nature often got him into difficulties. The school soon dismissed him because the administrators felt he was a troublemaker. Those who knew Ho said that even at this early age he was already developing political ideas that the French did not like.

Their country still occupied by foreigners, peasants near Hanoi in northern French Indochina operate a primitive treadmill device to irrigate rice fields in 1951. Rice was cultivated in this centuries-old manner well into the 20th century. Ho's revolutionary forerunner, Phan Boi Chau, had said, "The Vietnamese people as compared with Western people are still far behind."

A 1917 photograph of high mandarins, or public officials, in Annam province in colonial Vietnam. Ho's family moved from Nghe An province to Hué, Annam's capital, when he was eight years old. Ho's father, who took exams to become a mandarin, remarked: "Being a mandarin is the ultimate form of slavery."

A Buddhist pagoda leans in the jungle in Tonkin province, French Indochina. Buddhism was the leading religious system in the area before Catholic missionaries brought Christianity to Vietnam in the 17th century. Colonial administrators later promoted Catholicism over native faiths.

About this time, Nguyen Sinh Huy changed Ho's name to Nguyen Tat Thanh, which translates to "Nguyen Who Will Eventually Succeed." This new name was derived from Ho's steadfast belief in hard work and his intense desire to succeed. It was only the first of his many name changes throughout his life. Ho's father also changed his own name to Nguyen Tat Sac.

Two years later, Ho was enrolled in another school in Hué. At this time he was noticed as a bright young political thinker by his father's friend, the rebel Phan Boi Chau.

At the turn of the century the Japanese considered expanding their influence into what was then French Indochina. As a result, Japan opened its doors to Vietnamese rebels such as Phan Boi Chau between 1905 and 1908. From their haven in Japan, where the French could not reach them, Phan and others could incite the people to revolt.

Phan Boi Chau asked Ho to join him in a militant effort to oust the French. Phan had started a radical group in Japan called *Hoi Duy Tan*, or the Modernist Movement. In one of his anti-French articles Phan fiercely declared, "Those gray-eyed, heavily bearded people cannot live if Vietnam is to live!" The group hoped to restore the power of the old Vietnamese monarchy with the help of the Japanese.

Ho did not want to return to the old monarchy; he had more progressive ideas for the future of Vietnam. At age 15, he turned down Phan Boi Chau's offer.

Ho Chi Minh did indeed want to kick the French out of his country, but he had little confidence in Phan's group. Ho was suspicious of the Japanese, fearing they themselves would ultimately seek to subjugate the Vietnamese, just as the French had. Later, it was said of Ho: "He thought that to fight the French colonialists with the help of Japanese militarists would be to 'hunt the tiger only to be eaten by the wolves.' "

In 1906 the French governor of Ho's village ordered the mayors of the district to appear before him. He wanted to interrogate each one about the identities and whereabouts of Vietnamese rebel fighters. Ho went in place of his mayor, eager to stand up publicly against the French. He put all fears aside and spoke out vehemently against colonial policies. The governor, who wielded great power in his position and could easily have sent Ho to prison, was caught off guard by Ho's courage, and was too impressed to punish the boy. Ho's first confrontation with the enemy was a success.

In 1908 the French ordered the Scholars' movement's school closed and their activities stopped. Many members were jailed, including Ho's father, who, after his release, was sent out of Hué to Saigon in the south. There he set up a practice in Chinese medicine while under house arrest.

At 18, Ho was expelled from school for distributing copies of an anticolonialist paper, and he never received his degree. By 1909 Ho Chi Minh was ready to find his own method for liberating his country. Ho accepted this challenge and was ready to do what was necessary to gain freedom for his people.

French armor parades through Hanoi in Tonkin province to commemorate Bastille Day on July 14, France's most significant national celebration. On July 14, 1901, a half century before this parade took place, the French suppressed an uprising by Vietnamese rebels.

2

The Angry Patriot

After leaving school, Ho taught in an anti-French village in Cochin China. He quit teaching and moved to Saigon where he visited his father and entered a culinary school; Ho believed he needed a useful trade by which he could support himself during his future travels. The startling news of the overthrow of the monarchy in China caused Ho Chi Minh to leave the village in 1911. The revolution there had been organized by the Chinese rebel leader Sun Yat-sen and the Vietnamese patriot Phan Boi Chau in Japan. This revolt convinced Ho that only by having strong allies in other countries could such a rebellion be successful in Vietnam.

Once he had acquired skills in the art of cooking, Ho would spend the next two years, beginning in 1912, as a cook's assistant aboard a French merchant ship. Nguyen Tat Sac had advised his son to go to France, and Ho was able to get a job aboard the SS *La Touche-Tréville*, bound for Marseilles. With him, Ho carried a letter from his father's friends in the outlawed Scholars' movement to be delivered to Phan Chu Trinh, the organization's leader, then living in Paris. Ho soon realized that

EASTFOTO

Smiling schoolchildren at their desks in a bamboo school house in the early 1950s. Before Vietnam became a French colony in 1883–84, most Vietnamese could read and write. Attempts to replace the Vietnamese language with French increased illiteracy among the people.

This Roman Catholic cathedral in Hanoi, French Indochina, stands in stark contrast to the Southeast Asian society that surrounds it. Roman Catholic missionaries began converting Vietnamese to Christianity in the 17th century, thus forming the basis for French colonial rule. By the late 19th century, many Vietnamese, especially in the south, had become Catholics.

Vladimir Lenin, founder of the Soviet Union (the first nation based upon Marxist theories) and leader of the 1917 Bolshevik revolution. Lenin, whose ideas Ho studied while in Moscow, believed that "vanguard fighters," rather than the working class alone, were necessary to overthrow capitalism.

the movement's principles were not his own; he could not comprehend Phan Chu Trinh's plan to coexist peacefully with the French. After deciding to continue his seagoing travels, he returned briefly to Saigon. There his father, who had found out that Ho disagreed with Phan, drove his son away, brandishing a stick. Ho decided never to see his father again.

After his years aboard the French vessel, he became a cook at the Carlton, an expensive London hotel. Here Ho saw a society much like his own, with two classes of people — the wealthy and the poor. Ho joined the Overseas Workers' Association for foreign workers who were not allowed, because of their nationalities, to join the British trade unions.

World War I broke out in 1914. Ho signed up to

work aboard ships delivering supplies, ammunition, and other goods between England and the United States. He left the ship when it docked in New York, intending to learn all about this "land of the free," as he had heard it called. While in New York, Ho worked in kitchens and waited on tables. Ho's impression was that in America different classes had varying degrees of freedom, depending on their wealth.

Restless, Ho returned to Europe in 1917 amidst the grim days of World War I. Settling in Paris, he worked a variety of jobs until finding steady employment as a photo retoucher. This job did not supply him with much money, but it provided plenty of free time to study the philosophies of the French socialists. For the second time, Ho encountered Phan Chu Trinh, who helped Ho write the Eight Point Program he would take to Versailles.

Members of a Chinese Bomb Corps unit pose with their weapons in 1911. That year, such units helped rebels led by the Western-educated Sun Yat-sen overthrow the Chinese monarchy. Ho was greatly impressed by the Chinese Revolution, which was organized partly by Vietnamese independence fighter Phan Boi Chau.

Women in Annam, French Indochina, prepare silk worm cocoons for the unraveling of valuable silk. France frequently rationalized its colonial rule by claiming to bring modern industry, agriculture, and a higher standard of living to the Vietnamese people. But French monopolies, high taxes, and rents drove many peasants into poverty.

Surrounded by the poverty of the French working class and by liberal activists who sought to change the inequalities in society, Ho began an education that would mold him into one of the most famous revolutionaries of the 20th century. Ho became increasingly determined to make Vietnam an independent nation. With his exposure to radical politics, he began to study the economic forces that divided people into different classes, the various nations into empires and colonies. In Vietnam and in the other Asian countries where he had traveled, Ho had only met racist and arrogant colonial Frenchmen. Now in Paris he was spending time with French workers and thinkers who regarded him as being on an equal footing with themselves.

"He was," wrote the French scholar and journalist Jean Lacouture, "struck by the similarity between the lot of the exploited inhabitants of a colony and that of a European worker — and it was to this parallel . . . that he was to devote one of his earliest articles. No one could have felt more naturally drawn to organized labor and the parties of the left. Had Ho stayed home, he might never have progressed beyond an extremist form of nationalism. . . . Living immersed for a while in a hierarchical, industrialized society broadened his outlook and gave a political slant to his thought. Contact with the French Left was soon to turn an angry patriot into a modern revolutionary."

In 1920 Ho attended the French Socialist Party Congress held at Tours. There he joined the party's most extreme left wing — a term used to indicate

New York City's Fifth Avenue teems with automobiles and pedestrians in this 1929 photograph. In 1911 Ho left his teaching position in Cochin China (southern Vietnam) and went to culinary school in Saigon. Ho subsequently toured the world on a French merchant ship, worked as a cook in London, and, in 1914, came to New York, where he worked in restaurants and observed American society.

Marcel Cachin was the French Socialist party's representative to the Bolshevik Communist Congress of 1920 in Moscow. Cachin presented Soviet communist demands to the French Socialist Party Congress in Tours, France. At the Congress, Ho joined Cachin's more radical socialists, who formed the French Communist party.

Algerian anticolonialist Messali Hadj was the Muslim founder of the Star of North Africa, which aimed to upgrade working-class life throughout that region. The organization, established in 1923, became the *Parti Populaire Algérien* (the Algerian People's Party). In 1920 Ho Chi Minh and Messali Hadj published the anti-French newspaper *Le Paria (The Outcast)*.

groups desiring radical social reform — that at this very same meeting split off to form the French Communist party under the leadership of Marcel Cachin.

Soon after, Ho became a professional journalist, writing articles for the socialist daily paper *Le Populaire* and the French communist paper *L'Humanité*. He wrote persistently of the French capitalists' exploitation of the Vietnamese people.

In 1920 Ho, along with a fellow anticolonialist, Messali Hadj, from Algeria, published *Le Paria (The Outcast)*, a leftist, and decidedly anti-French, newspaper. He wrote under the pen name Nguyen Ai Quoc, or "Nguyen the Patriot."

Ho also helped found a Vietnamese revolutionary paper titled *Viet Nam Hon (The Soul of Vietnam)*. The aim of this paper was to arouse sympathy in places outside of France and her empire as well as encourage rebellion from within the colonies themselves. It was in this paper that Ho published his list of suggestions, his Eight Point Program that he had attempted to submit to President Wilson at the Versailles Peace Conference.

Ho wrote many articles criticizing French colonialism. His first substantial contribution to revolutionary literature, *Le Procès de la Colonisation Française (French Colonization on Trial)*, addressed the economic and social injustices inflicted by the Western rulers. In 30,000 words it condemned French conscription of Vietnamese into World War I, the introduction of alcohol into a nation that had never indulged in the habit of drinking, the promotion of the sale of the dangerous drug

With knives in their mouths, French Communist party demonstrators in Paris in 1920 lampoon anticommunist propaganda posters that portrayed communists as knife-wielding and treacherous. Ho Chi Minh was then writing for the socialist daily paper *Le Populaire* and the communist journal *L'Humanité*.

AP/WIDE WORLD

A street scene during the 1930s in the Chinese district of Hanoi, the largest city in Tonkin, the northernmost province of French-controlled Vietnam. The Chinese were both feared and admired in Vietnam. Vietnamese culture and political thought were extensively influenced by the Chinese.

opium, and the severe political and economic repression of the natives.

Colonial officials of French Indochina at first sought to extract resources and profit from their Vietnamese possessions, but to interfere very little in the people's way of life. These officials believed it was better simply to exploit the society rather than try to make it a French one. In the early 20th century, however, the French had begun to try to reshape Vietnamese culture. Certain more reformist administrators wanted to educate the people in democratic government and create what they called

A horse-drawn carriage on a cobbled street in the Soviet capital, Moscow, during the 1920s. In 1924 Ho traveled to the Soviet Union by train, using a falsified Chinese passport. While studying Marxism-Leninism in Moscow, Ho won favorable recognition from the Soviet-controlled communist organization, the Comintern, or Communist International.

Ho Chi Minh meets with the French press shortly after becoming president of the Democratic Republic of Vietnam on August 25, 1945. Having used numerous aliases, the revolutionary leader emerged after the 1945 Vietminh uprising as Ho Chi Minh ("Ho Who Aspires to Enlightenment").

Villagers at a bazaar in the French protectorate of Annam in 1917. Marketplaces where peasants bought and sold their wares were commonplace throughout Vietnam. Competitive economic practices and private ownership were unsuccessfully forced by the French upon the Vietnamese. To most of Ho's countrymen, a subsistence economy that provided food and shelter was sufficient.

an Indochinese Union. Although puppet legislatures were set up in Annam and Tonkin, based on an earlier Colonial Council in Cochin China, no "union" was ever established.

Vietnam had a farm-based economy that was disrupted by French attempts to increase agricultural production for commercial purposes. The Vietnamese people were not encouraged to start their own industries. Their labor was important to the manufacturing concerns owned by the French; the sale and consumption of salt, alcohol, and opium by the population earned money for French monopolies. Many peasants had to move to the cities, such as Hanoi, Haiphong, and Da Nang, when their labor was no longer needed in the rice paddies. Except for those who managed to find work in factories, many joined the ranks of a new urban poor.

After World War I, production of rice (Vietnam's chief export) was stepped up. In fact, as more rice was grown and sold abroad by the French, rice consumption by the Vietnamese population actually declined. Rubber soon became the second most important export from Vietnam. Three times as much land was devoted to growing rubber plants between 1917 and 1926 as had been the case prior to this time.

Ho's activities in the communist movement increased dramatically from 1920 to 1922. He visited Moscow in 1923, where he served as a French Communist party delegate to the Kresintern (the Peasants' International). This, together with subsequent journeys to Moscow, made a deep and lasting impression on Ho.

In a traditional opium den in colonial Vietnam, an opium user smokes a pipe containing the powerful and addictive narcotic. Use of opium was prevalent in China and Southeast Asia. The production of opium, which once had been sold to finance underground anti-French activities in Vietnam, was monopolized by the French in the 1930s.

3

Agent of the Revolution

*He was taut and quivering,
with only one thought in his
head, his country, Vietnam.*
—French communist, on Ho Chi
Minh during his years of exile

The Russian Revolution of October 1917 had resulted in the overwhelming victory of communism over the monarchical regime of the tsar. Vladimir Lenin, the leader of the revolution, and his communist political party, the Bolsheviks, embraced the doctrines of the 19th-century German philosopher and economist Karl Marx. In his writings, Marx discussed the relationship between the proletariat, or working class, and the capitalists. He predicted that the proletariat would ultimately overthrow the capitalists, resulting in a state of economic equality perpetuated by the working masses.

Ho Chi Minh read the works of Marx and Lenin and closely watched the political developments in Russia. He joined the Third International, a radical group headed by Lenin, which sought to liberate the oppressed workers worldwide. Now more than ever, Ho was impatient with the French; he felt the Third International might be a new answer to the ills of colonialism in Vietnam.

In his later years, Ho Chi Minh reflected on how the independence struggle became a matter of establishing communism in his country as well: "In

AP/WIDE WORLD

Karl Marx, the German-born socialist philosopher and economist. His analysis of history, revolution, and capitalism inspired the Russian Bolshevik Revolution (1917) and the Chinese Communist Revolution (1945–49). Ho effectively combined traditional Vietnamese ideas with those of Marx, emphasizing the group, not the individual.

Ho Chi Minh as president of the Democratic Republic of Vietnam. Shortly after Japan's surrender in August 1945, ending World War II, the Vietminh seized territory in northern Vietnam; on September 2, Ho proclaimed the region's independence. In the south, a so-called republic was set up in Cochin China by French Admiral Thiérry d'Argenlieu.

EASTFOTO

the beginning, it was patriotism and not communism which induced me to believe in Lenin and the Third International. But little by little, progressing step by step in the course of the struggle . . . I came to realize that socialism and communism alone are capable of emancipating workers and downtrodden people all over the world."

Lenin's ideas appealed to Ho because of their common beliefs. Lenin stated that only by acting as a group could the working classes win. Ho's own society was group-oriented; the Vietnamese people felt most comfortable when unified by a single cause. They wanted to be free of European control. Ho wanted to learn more about communist society and decided to go to Moscow.

After getting a fake Chinese passport — since the French would not allow the Vietnamese to travel in 1924 — Ho traveled by train into the Soviet Union. He spent most of the year studying in Moscow at the University of Oriental Workers. It was not long before his abilities were recognized by the Communist International (the Comintern), the worldwide communist organization that had evolved from the Russian Revolution.

While at the university in Moscow, Ho studied the methods of revolution developed by Lenin. The school stressed five basic rules: Start the revolution only when the fighters are dedicated completely to winning; choose the right place and make sure rebel troops there are stronger than the government's troops; choose the right time, such as when the government's forces are weak and scattered; convince the rebel forces that they are just in their cause; and always be aggressive.

Marx predicted that in the most industrialized countries workers would most likely develop an awareness of their situation. They would naturally become organized and begin the revolution. To Lenin, the truth of Marx's theories could be regarded as "one piece of steel." But Lenin did not think that gradual change would bring about a communist society — quick, violent revolution would.

In countries with very little industry, such as Lenin's Russia in the early 1900s — and Ho's Viet-

The very existence of Vietnam as a separate country, and the survival of the Vietnamese as a distinct people, must be regarded as a miracle, for which scores of historians have so far tried vainly to find a satisfactory explanation.
—JOSEPH BUTTINGER
Austrian historian

nam — Lenin stated that "an organization of revolutionaries" was necessary to seize power. Lenin believed in "vanguard fighters" to overthrow capitalism. The kind of leadership needed, he said, "is sometimes fulfilled by a dictator." Lenin maintained that leadership came from physical strength and the power to influence the people. He relied on the power of the group to give power to the individual; he believed that through group cooperation to attain goals, life would be better for the individual.

Ho learned to use these ideas to influence the Vietnamese peasants at home. Ho added an ingredient to Lenin's list of leadership qualities — a feature that was called *shu* by the Chinese sage Confucius (or Kung-fu-dzu). There is no exact English equivalent, but an approximate translation is *common heart* — a feeling of give and take among individuals with the awareness that all men are brothers. One chronicler of Ho's activities states, "Ho's instinct seems to have been to work from the heart rather than the head."

Ho was easily able to blend the Marxist-Leninist ideas he learned in Moscow with old and cherished Vietnamese traditions. His people believed in a close village life where the needs of the community were put before those of the individual. Religion had taught them that change would come from above. A divine source would lead them into a new era and it was their duty to accept this leadership. The Vietnamese people also had a deep dislike for the foreign invader. In all of this Ho found a base from which to lead a successful communist revolt. But Ho had witnessed the failure of Vietnamese revolts in the past. These rebellions were never led by a strong central command. Such strength would come from him in the future. Though he changed his policies many times, Ho never lost sight of his most central beliefs.

Because of his leadership qualities, Ho began to receive money from Moscow in 1924, providing him with funding to carry on his revolution. He no longer needed to work odd jobs, and instead could spend his time learning more, meeting with influential people, and slowly making his plans.

> *Military action without politics is like a tree without roots.*
> —HO CHI MINH

Ho traveled often between Paris and Moscow in 1924. He addressed the Fifth World Congress of the Communist International in Moscow that year. Speaking before communists assembled from around the world, Ho demanded they take definitive action in Asia — a demand he had presented to the socialists in Tours, France, in 1920.

Sun Yat-sen had served as the new Chinese Republic's president, but had been forced by the army to flee in 1913 to Japan. The military leader who took Sun's place had no clear plans for his government, but managed to demolish the democratic system Sun had set up. When the commander died in 1916, powerful warlords saw their chance to take over the country. Sun then understood that he would need an effective military in order to stop the warlords.

In 1922 he struck a bargain with the Communist International. The Comintern told Sun that he would not have to serve the goal of communism in China; it would, however, order the Chinese communists to fight alongside the Guomindang, the Chinese Nationalist party. Mikhail Borodin was assigned to coordinate and train the uneasy allies. The

With a portrait of Lenin behind him, a Bolshevik party organizer exhorts Soviet peasants in 1928, a year Ho spent partly in Moscow. Ho's study of Marxism-Leninism and Soviet institutions contributed to his organizing the *Thanh Nien*, the Association of Vietnamese Revolutionary Youth, in 1925 in Canton, China.

Soviet leadership did, in fact, hope to steer this revolution toward communism.

Under the alias of Vuong, Ho organized "cell groups" among the Vietnamese exiles he found in Canton in order to help the Chinese revolt. These "cells" were small groups of rebels initiated to ensure secrecy. A larger organization could thus be broken into smaller units or pieces, like a puzzle. They would prove hard to trace, hard to connect. If a rebel was captured and questioned by the enemy, he could betray only the members of his cell. In this way, the rest of the overall network would be safe. Using this method, Ho would be able to keep the French from finding out his plans for future uprisings.

As Borodin's political adviser, Ho also taught the students international communist theory and how to put it into practice. He demonstrated the use of propaganda — the influencing of popular opinion through images, slogans, and symbols. They acted out roles to teach themselves how to explain their mission to peasants. They learned to write propaganda and were free to criticize and be criticized at any time. Ho always taught in a comprehensive, but simple manner.

Meanwhile, his Soviet colleague Borodin taught guerrilla tactics at the Whampoa Military Academy

A demonstration during the Russian Revolution. Lenin's return to Russia during World War I brought a second revolution in 1917, toppling the noncommunist government that seized power earlier that year. Ho, then in Paris, met socialists who turned the "angry patriot into a modern revolutionary," according to journalist Jean Lacouture.

in Canton. Ho took part in these lessons and learned the strategy of stealth. He immediately recognized how important learning guerrilla warfare tactics would be. Ho understood that this was a way of defeating an opponent having heavy land artillery and superior air power.

In 1926 Ho began to establish a Vietnamese independence party in Canton. He demonstrated that nothing, not even old friends, was more important than the goal of national freedom. Two years earlier

Confucius, or Kung-fu-dzu, the father of Chinese philosophy. A moral and political philosopher, Confucius emphasized virtue and loyalty at all levels of society. Confucianism dominated Vietnamese education from feudal times until 1917. Ho was able to integrate Lenin's ideas on leadership with traditional Confucian teachings.

AP/WIDE WORLD

Soviet military adviser Mikhail Borodin (left) with General Yu Yui Lien of the rebel Chinese Guomindang party in 1927. In 1925, a year after addressing the Fifth Congress of the Communist International, Ho Chi Minh accompanied Borodin to China to advise Chiang Kaishek, the Guomindang's leader after Sun Yat-sen's death.

Ho's father's friend, the revolutionary Phan Boi Chau, founded, and became the leader of, a nationalist Vietnamese party modeled after the Guomindang. It was called the *Viet Nam Quoc Dan Dang*, or the Vietnam National People's party. The VNQDD was also based in Canton. Ho wanted to absorb these nationalists into his newly formed group. So he lured Phan away from Canton and gave the *Sûreté* (the French colonial police) an anonymous tip revealing the radical's whereabouts. Phan was arrested and sentenced to hard labor. According to Vietnamese historian Hoang Van Chi, Ho sold this information for 100,000 *piasters*.

Ho then persuaded all of Phan's group to join his new organization called *Thanh Nien*, the Association of Vietnamese Revolutionary Youth. The group published a newspaper that was not openly communist, dealing primarily with nationalist topics. This subtle move was necessary, for Ho realized that he needed to appeal to and include peasants, whose background was steeped in conservative tradition.

Ho's new goal was to achieve power through a two-stage revolution.

The first stage would be to appeal to the "most conscientious elements in every class," he stated. The second, more long-term, phase would lead to socialism after a steady process of economic and social change. Before either phase could begin, however, Ho had to unite all the rival anticolonial groups into a single strong organization.

Ho's plans to unite the Vietnamese nationalist movements were interrupted when he was forced to leave Canton in 1927. Phan Boi Chau's arrest deepened the nationalists' suspicion toward their would-be communist allies. When Chiang Kai-shek became leader of the Guomindang in 1927, he turned on the communists, whom he had distrusted from the outset. After successfully appealing to wealthy

A man in Hanoi in the late 1930s carries bundles of sticks on shoulder poles — a method to which Ho himself was not accustomed when he journeyed on foot to Siam (now Thailand) in 1928. Hanoi became the capital of the Democratic Republic of Vietnam in 1954.

An elaborate Buddhist temple in Bangkok, Siam. Assuming the name Thau Chin, Ho walked to Udon, Siam, near Laos, in 1928, to visit exiled Vietnamese rebels. Having started both a newspaper and a school, Ho suddenly donned the monk's yellow robes and joined a Buddhist monastery.

Chinese bankers for financial support, Chiang attempted to wipe out the communists.

As the Chinese Communist party fled from the cities to the countryside, a young party organizer began his rise to prominence. A radical who wanted to turn China's peasant masses into a vast revolutionary movement, he had twice been denounced by the party's ruling committee. He argued that successful revolution in China depended on the peasantry, and not the workers in the cities. His name was Mao Zedong.

In a last-ditch attempt to maintain a foothold in China, Borodin offered Soviet assistance to an old follower of Sun's, Wang Ching-wei, to oppose Chiang. But Wang saw little possibility of winning and laid down his arms. Borodin and Ho were in danger. Ho fled Canton, taking a boat to the Soviet port of Vladivostok; then he rode the Trans-Siberian

Sun Yat-sen founded the Guomindang, or Nationalist, party, which sought to bring constitutional and democratic government to China. He served briefly as president of the Chinese Republic after the Manchu monarchy was overthrown in 1911. Rebel Phan Boi Chau's VNQDD (Vietnamese Nationalist party) was modeled after Sun's party in the 1930s.

railroad across the vast Soviet territory to Moscow.

In Moscow he was immediately contacted by the Comintern, who quickly dispatched him to Europe. Ho spent his time in Western countries, improving his public speaking skills and learning more about the imperial powers. In the meantime, some of his students from Canton had gone back into Vietnam and were forming cells. Ho's plans were starting to take shape.

In 1928 Ho traveled to northern Siam (now called Thailand), and adopted a new alias, Thau Chin. He made the journey to visit the Vietnamese in exile. He made this trip on foot. Although he was older than his companions, he walked the rocky and difficult path for 10 days. One of the travelers recalled, "Each of us had to carry two boxes of clothes, a cutlass, a bamboo tube full of salted chicken or pork and ten kilos of rice. Seeing that Mr. Chin was not accustomed to carrying things on shoulder-poles we offered to take his boxes, but he refused. After two or three days, we found that his feet were swollen and bleeding. But he smiled, saying they would soon get used to it. Indeed, after the fourth day, Mr. Chin was able to follow the rest of us quite well."

One of the first things Ho did once he reached Udon, Siam, was to begin a school. He also started a newspaper, much as he had done in Canton. He was safe from the French Sûreté here, but daily life was very difficult.

Ho's life took a different turn at this point. He moved into a monastery in Bangkok. He put on the robe of the Buddhist monks and used the time for spiritual needs as well as for preaching Marxism. (The Buddhists would later prove important in opposing pro-Western regimes in Vietnam.) This peaceful existence lasted for a year, until a crisis developed among the Vietnamese communists.

Rival Vietnamese communist groups became suspicious of each other's aims and ended up forming three separate parties while Ho was in the monastery. All said they represented Vietnamese communism and, at the time, each of the three groups made its main headquarters in the British colony of Hong Kong.

Near the end of 1929, the Comintern became alarmed by this party infighting and sent a message instructing Ho to intervene. Ho gave up his monk's robe and left the monastery.

On February 3, 1930, Ho met the leaders of the three factions in a secret congress during a soccer match at the Hong Kong stadium. The unification of the Vietnamese communists was difficult and some fought strongly for their beliefs. Ho's diplomatic skills were severely tested, but he finally pulled the groups together, along with the Association of Vietnamese Revolutionary Youth, into one party, the Vietnamese Communist party. (The name was soon changed in 1931 to the Indochinese Communist party, or ICP, to include potential members from neighboring countries.)

Ho was able to design the party's aims so they would have a broad appeal to the people throughout French Indochina; the region included not only An-

Buddhist priests in northern Siam, during the period when Ho Chi Minh joined a monastery there. Ho spent a year among the priests to put French colonial police off his trail, and win Buddhist monks over to Marxism; such monks actively opposed subsequent pro-Western regimes in South Vietnam.

nam, Tonkin, and Cochin China, but also Laos and Cambodia. Although the party had a new name, the organization was to be based in Vietnam. He realized that without the support of the people, a leader would not have any significant, long-term power. The goals of the ICP, as outlined by Ho, were the overthrow of French colonialism; the independence of Indochina; the establishment of a government of workers, peasants, and soldiers; the institution of an eight-hour working day; the improvement of education; freedom of speech, press and assembly; and equality of the sexes. The party approved the confiscation of large plantations and banks in Vietnam. This often involved taking control of the businesses through force.

By the mid-1920s, Vietnam's small number of modern workers totaled about 200,000. They worked in the French-owned coal mines, factories, and shipping industries. In Saigon, Cochin China, some of the dock workers had begun secretly to form labor unions. When the Great Depression (the economic crisis triggered by the United States' stock market crash in 1929) sent shock waves through the European economy, the French shut down many plants in Vietnam. The loss of jobs caused unrest in the cities, and on the rubber plantations. This small "proletariat" also began to strike for higher wages and better working conditions.

The same year brought about the most violent nationalistic uprising Vietnam had seen in over 30 years. The Viet Nam Quoc Dan Dang (its name meant Guomindang in Vietnamese) had remained outside Ho's influence. Members of the VNQDD believed the only way to liberate the Vietnamese people was to overthrow the French in an immediate revolution. In February 1930 the VNQDD members sparked a mutiny at Yen Bay, a French colonial fort manned by Vietnamese troops. The VNQDD infiltrated the troops and led them to mutiny against their officers. Several officers were killed, but the French had somehow been warned and were able to capture most of the VNQDD leaders. Captured VNQDD rebels were subsequently put to death by the guillotine. Some of the rebels escaped to the nearby village of Con An, but the French air force bombed and strafed the entire village, indiscriminately slaughtering innocent villagers as well as fleeing rebels. The VNQDD had moved too fast and did not sufficiently plan the attack. While this defeat for the VNQDD severely weakened the nationalist group, it cleared the way for Ho's Indochinese Communist party. Now the leadership of Vietnamese nationalism, the people's desire to be free to determine their own future, was in the hands of the communists.

On September 12, 1930, the ICP made an impressive display of power. Under their direction, 6,000 peasants in northern Annam made a march on Vinh, the provincial capital of Nghe Tinh. They seized several large estates and redistributed them into people's soviets, or highly disciplined collective organizations originally devised by Russian communists. This massive action greatly frightened and provoked the French colonials. They were shocked by the ICP's ability to mold the discontent of the peasantry into a viable threat to French supremacy in the region. The French quickly crushed the uprising. Among the rebels was one of the ICP's most prominent members, Pham Van Dong, later to become Ho's prime minister. Although Ho had no direct involvement in the affair (he was in Shanghai, China), the French sentenced him to death.

In 1931 Ho was named the head of the communist Far Eastern Bureau of the Comintern in the Soviet Union. This honor made Ho Moscow's official am-

Chiang Kai-shek succeeded Sun Yat-sen as leader of the Guomindang party in 1925. Ho, who organized the Association of Revolutionary Vietnamese Youth in Canton, China was forced to flee to Moscow in 1927 when Chiang's nationalists grew hostile toward the communists, whose strength had become concentrated in parts of China.

51

bassador to the communist movement in Southeast Asia.

In order to continue his subversive activities, Ho once again adopted a new name. This time he called himself Tang Van So. Nonetheless, Ho was arrested for the first time, at the age of 41. In cooperation with the French Sûreté, the British colonial police grabbed him in Hong Kong, intending to extradite him to Vietnam to be executed for the Vinh uprising. But after his capture, in an unexpected turn of events, Ho was kept in Hong Kong to face British charges. While in the Hong Kong prison, he became extremely ill with tuberculosis and was transferred to a prison hospital. After being permitted to leave prison, Ho traveled to Singapore in 1932. There he was arrested again, and returned to Hong Kong. At this point, the ICP was still surviving despite attempts by the French to crush it. Ho gained his freedom when a British anti-imperialist sympathizer smuggled him out of the hospital. Strangely, the British released reports in 1933 that Ho (then calling himself Nguyen Ai Quoc) had died in prison. The newspapers and the French Sûreté were all convinced that Ho was really dead.

Jean Lacouture noted that more than a decade

Sun Yat-sen with his wife. Sun's Guomindang party stood for ridding China of a monarchical dynasty and foreign domination. Sun, like Ho, was influenced by Western political ideas, but the Chinese nationalists soon clashed with communists after Sun's death. In 1933, disguised as a businessman, Ho obtained funds from the widowed Madame Sun Yat-sen for a journey to Moscow.

THE BETTMANN ARCHIVE

Ho Chi Minh with Soviet soldier and politician Marshal Kliment Voroshilov (in light suit) in Moscow, before attending talks in Geneva, Switzerland. The resulting treaty divided Ho's nation into North and South Vietnam in 1954.

later one French high official, upon receiving continuous messages from his intelligence agents on Nguyen Ai Quoc, and covert activities, answered back: "What kind of lunatic is sending us information like that? Everyone knows Nguyen Ai Quoc died in Hong Kong in the early thirties. . . ." Ho's communist and nationalist supporters mourned his passing. Meanwhile, Ho was out of Hong Kong on his way north to the Chinese port of Amoy.

During the next two years Ho lived as a merchant in Amoy, China. Later, in 1933, the Comintern learned that Ho was still alive and asked him to return to Moscow. In order to get money for the journey, he contacted the widow of the Chinese rebel Sun Yat-sen.

Ho posed as a wealthy businessman to get by the guards at the palace where Madame Sun Yat-sen lived. She gave him the money secretly because she too was under watch, and Ho was soon on his way to Moscow. On his arrival he was surprised how much Moscow had changed since his earlier visits.

4

Citizen of a Lost Country

All subject peoples are filled with hope by the prospect that an era of right and justice is opening for them in the struggle of civilization against barbarism.
—HO CHI MINH

Wen Lenin died suddenly in January 1924, Joseph Stalin became dictator of the Soviet Union. He ruled through terror. Not even his closest advisers were safe from his fears of enemies. Secret police stamped out the slightest flicker of opposition. In the dead of night they stormed into the homes of Soviet citizens accused of being subversives. Arrested on trumped-up charges, many disappeared into labor camps or were executed. It was later discovered that Stalin was responsible for the murder of millions of Russians — most of them innocent.

Ho realized the Russian Revolution had taken a fateful turn and he accepted it. He returned to the Lenin Institute in 1934, where he studied quietly for a year. Stalin became aware of the Vietnamese revolutionary in 1935, when Ho appeared as a delegate at the Seventh World Congress of the Communist International. Ho spoke for allowing the party to support any group that was in opposition to fascism (the political movement that emerged with the rise of the dictators Mussolini in Italy and Hitler in Germany).

Ho Chi Minh with two children who presented him with flowers on the second anniversary of the founding of the Lao Dong, or Vietnamese Labor party, a name first used by the Vietnamese communists in 1951. Its slogan, "The anti-imperialist and the anti-feudalist fights are of equal importance," indicated that both defeating the French and changing the economic system were considered necessary by the organization.

THE BETTMANN ARCHIVE

Léon Blum, politician, writer, and first Socialist premier of France from 1936 to 1937. Blum wrote for the journal *L'Humanité* and founded the socialist daily *Le Populaire*, to which Ho contributed. As premier, Blum was lenient toward Vietnamese political activity — legalizing the Indochinese Communist party, and freeing Vietnamese political prisoners.

In a fascist state, one leader with absolute power makes policy for the country. Fascist governments are ruled by a single elite party. Basic political and social freedoms do not exist under fascism. The dictator manipulates the population with violent nationalist goals, shows of military power, and often myths of superior and inferior races. Terror and brutality are used to enforce the dictator's will. Just prior to World War II, the world saw fascist regimes come to power in Italy, Germany, and Japan.

It was Ho's stand against the fascists, and his hopes of uniting everyone against them, that angered Stalin. Stalin did not want the Communist party in Moscow to ally with anyone who was not under his direct control. Stalin's fear of conspiracy grew worse with each passing day. When Stalin saw dissension or lack of support in groups such as Ho's ICP, they were destroyed. Ho's group somehow managed to stay alive.

The Indochinese Communist party grew in numbers and strength while its membership continued to shape the party's ideas and policies. At its first congress, Ho had developed a set of policies that he wanted the impatient young revolutionaries to follow. Ho wanted two major revisions to be adopted by the ICP. First, with the world in danger of total war, Ho emphasized that now was not the time to declare national independence. The ICP should seek only its own legalization. Second, in order to achieve this simple political freedom the ICP must communicate with a broad range of people, not just those sympathetic to the revolutionaries. Thus Ho expanded the ICP to include not only Indochinese people seeking independence, but also people from France living in Indochina who believed in the rights of the Vietnamese. He was stressing as much cooperation as possible between all sectors of Indochinese society, especially other leftist groups.

When a socialist government led by Léon Blum came to power in France in 1936, political conditions improved somewhat for Vietnamese radicals. This government was known as the Popular Front, a short-lived coalition between French socialists and communists. Premier Blum ordered the legal-

If they force us into war, we will fight. The struggle will be atrocious, the Vietnamese people will suffer anything rather than renounce their freedom.

—HO CHI MINH

ization of the ICP and the release of political prisoners, such as Pham Van Dong. A spirit of cooperation seemed possible between the French and Vietnamese. For the first time, Vietnamese communists no longer kept their existence a secret. But French prejudice soon forced the ICP back underground by 1937.

In the meantime, Chiang Kai-shek's nationalist forces and Mao Zedong's communists were separately fighting the Japanese, who had just invaded China. In 1939 Mao, then the chairman of the Chinese Communist party, and Chiang joined forces upon the suggestion of the Soviet Union. The Comintern sent Ho into the area as a political commissar. In order to travel undetected through the Japanese-held territory, Ho dressed as a beggar, and pushed a cart through the countryside. By the time he arrived at Mao's headquarters of huts and caves in Yenan, Ho had once again succumbed to tuberculosis.

After several months of recuperation, Mao sent him to the south of China to train Chiang's troops in the art of guerrilla warfare. Ho used this opportunity to train his own men and to establish a base close to the Vietnamese border.

Ho set up a training camp at Liuchow, China. There he met Pham Van Dong, to whom he had

From left to right: Joseph Stalin, Vladimir Lenin, and Mikhail Kalinin, one of Stalin's political lieutenants. After Lenin's death, Stalin became dictator of the Soviet Union. Stalin ruled by terror, destroying real and alleged opponents within the communist movement at home and abroad. Ho's Indochinese Communist party managed to survive.

taught revolutionary tactics in Canton. He also made a new acquaintance, Vo Nguyen Giap.

Giap had been educated at the prestigious Sorbonne, at the University of Paris. He had been a professor of French military history at the University of Hanoi and had written a manual on guerrilla warfare, *People's War, People's Army*. Years later, Giap would prove to be one of the world's most cunning military strategists.

Ho often wandered to small villages, selling a self-published newspaper to Chinese railroad workers. He had little money and was in poor health, but he continued on his mission. The Chinese imprisoned him a second time, rendering him thinner and weaker than before. This was an extremely difficult period for Ho. Yet, during his convalescence, he watched and listened to what was happening in the world. He realized his revolutionary activities would depend enormously upon the outcome of World War II. Ho accurately predicted that the Japanese would become embroiled in a war with the United States and be defeated.

In 1940, Germany captured France and the Japanese occupied Vietnam. Vietnamese writer Hoang Van Chi has said that World War II "severed contact between France and Vietnam." The Japanese took much of the power away from the French colonists living in Vietnam. Ho decided not to oppose the Japanese directly. Instead, he moved his communist organization from the border back into Vietnam.

Ho's group settled in Bac Bo, an area of natural limestone caves, not far from the border. Ho patterned his life as Mao Zedong had while he was preparing his troops in China. Ho was always busy working, holding meetings, studying, or visiting nearby villages. He educated the villagers in politics, and showed village children how to read and write. The nights were often too cold to sleep. On such nights "Uncle" Ho and his fellow revolutionaries stayed awake, huddled around a fire the entire night, listening as Ho recounted the development of revolutions in other parts of the world. As a symbol of respect to those who had had the most influence on him, Ho named a nearby peak Karl Marx

[The French] may stay for a while, but they will have to go because the white man is finished in Asia.

—HO CHI MINH

The Sorbonne, part of the University of Paris. Vo Nguyen Giap, Vietminh army commander-in-chief and Ho's defense minister, studied law here. Sent in 1938 by the Comintern to advise nationalist and communist troops fighting the Japanese in China, Ho met Giap, who had been a communist since 1930.

Mao Zedong (left) confers with Ho Chi Minh in Beijing, China, in 1955. Ho first encountered the Chinese communist leader in 1939 at Mao's headquarters in Yenan, China. The Comintern sent Ho to advise Mao's communists and Chiang's nationalists in their cooperative fight against the Japanese. Mao sent Ho to southern China to train Chiang's soldiers.

Mountain and a brook Lenin Stream. Those who were with him at this time contributed to the communist independence movement's next form: the *Viet-Nam Doc-Lap Dong Minh*, or the League for the Independence of Vietnam. The name was later shortened to Vietminh.

In this mountain hamlet, a new government was planned by the ICP Central Committee in May 1941. Ho named their program *Cuu Quoc*, or National Salvation, from which would come National Salvation Associations. These associations organized peasants, women, students, and workers. They proclaimed: "After the overthrow of the Japanese fascists and the French imperialists, a revolutionary government of the Democratic Republic of Vietnam will be set up in the new democracy; its emblem will be the red flag with a gold star." Emphasizing nationalism instead of Marxist-Leninist politics, Ho realized the new organization would command greater appeal than the ICP. To further demonstrate that he was putting Vietnamese nationalism before communism, on his 51st birthday, he dropped all aliases associated with his communist activities and adopted the name Ho Chi Minh, "Ho Who Aspires to Enlightenment." With guerrilla units training in the mountains for the struggle's next phase, the Vietminh would pounce as soon as the Pacific war was over. This initial guerrilla organization would be the prototype for the Vietnamese Liberation Army.

When the time had come to announce the group's existence to the world, Ho smuggled himself back into China. In June 1941 Ho made a radio broadcast from China that quickly became famous through-

Who are the masters? Our people are! Our countrymen are! Wake up! Wake up!
—PHAN BOI CHAU
Vietnamese nationalist

Vo Nguyen Giap (left) with Ho Chi Minh in September 1945. A former professor of French military history at the University of Hanoi, Giap joined the Indochinese Communist party at its inception. After fighting the Japanese, Giap successfully led Vietminh troops against France's campaign, begun in 1946, to reconquer northern Vietnam.

61

out all of Vietnam. The message was spread by word of mouth through the peasant villages of Vietnam. Ho stated: "If our entire people are united and single-minded, we can smash the targeted French and Japanese armies. . . . Let us unite together! Victory to the World revolution! Victory to the Vietnamese revolution!"

It is important to realize that despite his bold words, Ho made no attempt to spark an uprising. The Japanese were still too strong in Vietnam, and any uprisings that did occur were quickly and violently suppressed.

Things changed one short month after the official formation of the Vietminh — Germany attacked the Soviet Union on June 22. At long last, defeating the fascists became a top communist priority. Ho realized it was time to take action.

The villages were prepared for a move against the Japanese because Ho had been sending propaganda

Ho speaks before Soviet officials. During World War II the Soviets granted Ho's Vietnamese independence movement little support. When the Japanese army invaded Vietnam in 1940, French influence there disintegrated, allowing Ho to form the nationalist Vietminh in 1941, which infiltrated Vietnam from the Chinese border.

units into the villages to explain the situation, and what needed to be done to save the country. Giap began to show his military genius when he devised a strategy which would help the Vietnamese overcome their greatest disadvantage — a lack of military arms.

One of the key points in Giap's strategy was that his forces were to be flexible. His plan of attack would vary according to the individual situation. Typically striking and retreating into the jungle, Giap was able to create an elusive front line that mystified his opponents. He formulated a plan to help the Vietminh overcome its lack of weapons while continuing to hamper the enemy. Giap decided that his forces should attack the small colonial outposts behind enemy lines where supplies and ammunition were stored. Giap had extensively studied European history. He also knew that a large force cut off from its supplies could not continue to

The city of Hanoi as it appeared in 1940 when the Japanese military planned to annex European colonies in Southeast Asia as part of a "Greater East Asia Co-prosperity Sphere." Five years later, Ho's Vietminh stormed Hanoi after Japan's surrender to the Allies, and established a provisional government.

fight. By attacking the enemy from behind and keeping them from their supplies, the Vietminh could hardly lose.

Giap's soldiers carried very little so as to move easily through the jungle. They carried food and provisions enough only for a few days, foraging for food in the jungle whenever possible. Their basic uniforms consisted of sandals, a lightweight shirt, a pair of cotton pants, and a gun. By contrast, the

A Vietnamese woman guerrilla fighter who distinguished herself for valor in more than 30 combat missions against French colonial troops. Both men and women joined the Vietminh. Ho intended the organization to more clearly represent nationalist aims than the earlier Indochinese Communist party.

EASTFOTO

French troops were overloaded with equipment, thus lacking the mobility that became the Vietminh's chief weapon. Giap had found a working strategy and Ho was pleased.

Since the Russians were occupied with fighting the Germans, Ho was no longer able to communicate with the leadership in Moscow. The Communist International could no longer advise him; the Chinese communists were committed to the war against the Japanese. In addition, they were disappointed when Ho formed the more nationalist Vietminh. They rebuked him by refusing him help. Ho was now on his own.

Nazi Germany's Adolf Hitler and Fascist Italy's Benito Mussolini were dictators of their two nations. Behind them (left to right) are German Field Marshal Hermann Göring and Italian Foreign Minister Count Galeazzo Ciano. Mussolini's and Hitler's governments concentrated political, economic, and military power in the hands of a single ruler.

5

The Army in the Shadows

Without the support of Mao and Stalin, Ho had not only lost advisers, but also financial backing. In an attempt to find new funding for his revolution Ho turned to Chiang Kai-shek in China. Masquerading as a Chinese reporter in order to enter China, Ho was discovered and arrested. His capture was the result of collaboration between warlord Chang Fa-kwei, who now headed the VNQDD, and Guomindang leader Chiang Kai-shek. By imprisoning the Vietnamese communist, Chiang hoped to revive the pro-Guomindang VNQDD and keep the Vietminh from gaining power in Vietnam.

For the second time, a false message was sent to Ho's followers saying that he had died in prison. Hearing this, the Vietminh moved its headquarters deeper into Vietnam while mourning the loss of their leader. Eventually Ho was able to get a message out of prison that said he was still alive, but his friends were unable to get a release or effect an escape. Ho suffered greatly in the Chinese prison. His only consolation was the record he kept while imprisoned, subsequently published as the *Prison Di-*

Ho Chi Minh was called "Uncle" by many who worked with him. Isolated from Mao Zedong's Chinese communists and from Stalin, who had known of him since 1935, Ho ventured, in disguise, into China to seek Chiang Kai-shek's assistance in 1942. The pro-Guomindang Vietnamese Nationalist party (VNQDD) saw to Ho's capture, arrest, and imprisonment.

American Major General Claire L. Chennault commanded the "Flying Tigers," a volunteer fighter plane group which fought Japanese airpower over China. Showing a signed portrait of the respected general, Ho regained the Vietminh leadership by appearing to have earned Chennault's support.

THE BETTMANN ARCHIVE

ary. The diary consists of 120 poems, written in classical Chinese ideograms, detailing his sufferings and philosophical insights.

Ho's captors, who kept their prisoner in manacles, offered him his freedom if he agreed to work for them. Ho flatly refused. He remained steadfast for more than a year. Finally he consented to head the *Dong Minh Hoi*, or the Vietnam Revolutionary League. This new group was formed by the Chinese Guomindang to encompass all of the Vietnamese independence groups. Like the Guomindang, it was both anticommunist and anti-Japanese. However, this group was ineffective even with Ho as its leader. The Vietminh stayed intact despite Ho's long absence. It had been hoped by its enemies that the Vietminh would disintegrate if cut off from its charismatic leader. Ho eventually resigned from the Dong Minh Hoi in March 1944 and returned to the Vietminh.

Ho continued to make plans. During his incarceration in China, the Japanese jailed most of the French colonists. Early in 1945 the Japanese learned that the French colonial administration was plotting a counterattack against the invaders. They rounded up every French official they could find; French resistance plans had been smashed. Vo Nguyen Giap saw a chance to fight the Japanese. Recognizing the Japanese as the "common enemy," the Vietminh could assist Frenchmen against them, thus allowing the Vietminh to blend in with the Allied common front to defeat Japan.

Ho realized that with the French now powerless, and the Japanese losing the war against the Allies, there would soon be a political vacuum in Vietnam. Ho wanted the Vietminh forces to be ready to fill this void and take over the leadership of the country.

About a week after returning to the Vietminh, Ho met with an American intelligence officer in China. At first this officer regarded "Old Man Ho," as he called him, as only another anti-Japanese informer. Ho told the officer, Charles Fenn, how his men had rescued an American pilot who had been shot down by the Japanese and who had landed in the jungles of the north. He also told him that he headed the

Fortunately
Being stubborn and patient,
never yielding an inch,
Though physically I suffer, my
spirit is unshaken.
—HO CHI MINH
poem from the *Prison Diary*

largest anti-Japanese force in Vietnam — and that the Vietminh had declared Japan as its one and only enemy. Ho avoided telling Fenn that he was a communist. The OSS intelligence agency (subsequently called the CIA) investigated and found that French sources listed Ho as a communist.

When asked what supplies his troops needed, Ho said that they needed medicine, weapons, and radios. Once his organization had supplies it would let the American forces know where the Japanese were in Vietnam. The Vietminh could also help rescue more lost Allied pilots shot down over Vietnam.

It was at their second meeting that Ho asked Fenn for more supplies and if he could arrange a meeting with General Claire L. Chennault, who was stationed at a United States base in China. General

A portrait of Sun Yat-sen behind him, Chiang Kai-shek makes an anticommunist speech before members of the Guomindang in 1948, when his nationalist troops were attempting to annihilate the Chinese communists. Chiang imprisoned Ho, hoping to force Ho's cooperation and to rebuild the VNQDD. Chiang also circulated false reports of Ho's death.

American fighter aircraft of the famed "Flying Tigers" air group that helped defend Chiang Kai-shek's forces against the superior Japanese air force. Of Chennault, the unit's leader, British Prime Minister Winston Churchill said, "Well, thank God he's on our side."

Chennault was known in the East for his group of volunteer fighter pilots, the "Flying Tigers." These men had helped successfully defend civilians in Chinese cities from Japanese bomber attacks. Fenn gave Ho weapons and radios along with an American adviser to train Ho's forces. In 1945 Ho was even granted an appointment to meet the general.

Ho's meeting with the general went well; his simple charm impressed Chennault, who, having become acquainted with Eastern customs, was very courteous to his visitor. Ho looked much older than his 55 years. He proved to be well informed, and he complimented the general and the Flying Tigers. Ho asked Chennault for a memento — an autographed picture of the general. Chennault was flattered and gave Ho the picture, never suspecting how Ho would use it.

After many weeks of traveling over rugged terrain, Ho went to the new Vietminh headquarters in Lam Son. It was a 300-mile journey and he had walked a large part of the way. His friends were glad to see him, but were shocked to see how much his health had suffered.

Before Ho could organize the troops to take action, he became ill and was in a coma for a week. Slowly he recovered, but while he was regaining his health, rival leaders had come forward in the Vietminh group. Most of them were anti-Japanese resistance fighters, who had not been trained or educated in Ho's Marxist-Leninist ideology. None of them were as organized or experienced as Ho. He cleverly won back the loyalty of the Vietminh members.

Some time earlier he had asked Fenn to put away six new automatic pistols for him at the officer's

All those who do not follow the line which I have laid down will be broken.
—HO CHI MINH

Two Vietminh soldiers man an antiaircraft gun from their jungle outpost. In 1944 Vietminh guerrillas, trained under Ho's direction, would comprise the People's Liberation Army, which fought the Japanese during the last year of World War II.

EASTFOTO

Ho Chi Minh's portrait on view next to that of Chinese communist leader Mao Zedong, shortly after the Democratic Republic of Vietnam was established. When the French ultimately refused to recognize Ho's provisional government, leading to war in late 1946, Mao was unable to help Ho until the Chinese communists triumphed over the Guomindang in 1949.

Vo Nguyen Giap as deputy prime minister and minister of national defense of the Democratic Republic of Vietnam. His celebrated and startling victory over the French army at Dien Bien Phu in 1954 halted the French effort to regain Vietnam as a colony, and forced the French to negotiate an accord with Ho's government at Geneva, Switzerland.

headquarters. Ho now asked for the pistols, and when they arrived he showed them to the top leaders along with the autographed picture of General Chennault. The photo had been signed, "Yours Sincerely, Claire L. Chennault." The men believed that the general had sent Ho the guns personally, and that Ho had managed to get the Americans to supply them. From then on, Ho was the only leader.

While Ho was recovering, his military expert Giap was improving the Vietminh's combat readiness. He had formed an alliance with the mountain people known as the Thon, who were excellent guerrilla fighters. By December 1944, Giap was intending to use Thon mountain warriors as backup troops.

They formed the first platoon of the People's Liberation Army.

Only now, supplied with American-made rifles and radios, would Ho give Giap the go-ahead to send the troops against the Japanese. Germany had been defeated in May 1945, and Ho was not certain if the Japanese would prolong the war or surrender quickly. This question was answered when the United States dropped two atomic bombs on Japan and ended the war. On August 10, 1945, the day after the second bomb was dropped, the Japanese began retreating from Vietnam. Japan was ready to seek peace with the Western nations, and surrendered on August 15.

Commander-in-chief of the Vietminh armed forces Vo Nguyen Giap reviews his troops in 1952. With such soldiers, Giap tried to drive French troops from the China-Vietnam border in 1950. French forces, commanded by General Jean-Marie-Gabriel de Lattre de Tassigny, struck back with air attacks.

EASTFOTO

Ho Chi Minh cuts an Annamese cake at a conference held for French reporters after announcing his presidency of the Democratic Republic of Vietnam. On September 2, 1945, Ho proclaimed Vietnam's independence, drawing in his speech from the United States' Declaration of Independence and the French Declaration of the Rights of Man.

UPI/BETTMANN NEWSPHOTOS

We must always remember to fulfill our responsibilities as citizens of a lost country.
—HO CHI MINH

When the Japanese pulled out, the French, as Ho had foreseen, were too weak to take over. Vietnam was left without leaders. Ho had to act quickly before another group seized power. In two weeks time, the Vietminh had emerged as visibly in control in village after village.

One immediate obstacle was Vietnam's emperor, Bao Dai, who was favored by the upper classes. Bao Dai's reign had begun under the French in 1932. After the French colonial apparatus was dismantled in March 1945, Bao Dai was merely a figurehead used by the Japanese to pacify the Vietnamese people. With World War II over, the emperor was still considered a symbol of national independence to wealthy anticommunists.

On August 17, 1945, more than 100,000 people gathered for a political rally sponsored by the emperor in celebration of the defeat of the Japanese. The emperor's political allies spoke first. Then as Bao Dai took the podium, the red Vietminh flag appeared throughout the crowd and on the platform. A Vietminh spokesman leapt to the foreground. Turning to the crowd, he declared that the time had come for the Vietminh to lead. Only a truly revolutionary group could prevent foreign powers from taking control of Vietnam. "Let us unite together in a single bloc. The independence of the fatherland can be won only by blood. . . . We must take arms and rise up."

Revolutionary fervor was in the air. The people responded with parades and rallies — Vietminh

Members of the Vietminh's People's Army of Vietnam (PAVN) prepare to go into battle. While Ho strived to reach a settlement with France, Admiral Thiérry d'Argenlieu tried to create a separate state in Cochin China which, along with the French bombardment of Haiphong in November 1946, made war inevitable.

EASTFOTO

Vietnam's last monarch, Emperor Bao Dai. From 1932, when he began his reign, until August 1945, when Ho Chi Minh forced his abdication, Bao Dai was virtually powerless. French governors and World War II Japanese occupiers made Bao Dai a political figurehead.

AP/WIDE WORLD

flags and propaganda banners flew along major boulevards of Hanoi, Saigon, and Hué. The tide had turned; the people themselves now possessed a means to determine their country's future.

Anticipating that the French might send troops to his country to stop the revolutionary Vietminh, Bao Dai sent a telegram to the French military leader Charles de Gaulle with some prophetic advice: "You could understand even better if you were able to see what is happening here, if you were able to sense the desire for independence that has been smoldering in the bottom of all hearts, and which no human force can any longer hold back. Even if you were to arrive to reestablish a French administration here, it would no longer be obeyed; each village would be a nest of resistance, every former friend an enemy, and your officials and colonials themselves would ask to depart from this unbreathable atmosphere."

General Charles de Gaulle led the Free French movement in exile against the Nazis and the collaborationist French Vichy government during World War II. As de Gaulle's popularity grew throughout France in the late 1940s, French negotiators refused to consider Ho's demands for Vietnamese independence.

6

Path to Freedom

While the Vietminh was gaining national attention, Ho was waiting in seclusion. He watched international diplomacy closely: It seemed his hopes that Vietnam would be recognized worldwide as a sovereign nation were crumbling. In July 1945, a month before World War II ended in final victory for the Allies over Nazi Germany and Japan, the Allied powers met in Potsdam, Germany, and agreed to restore certain colonies to their owners. (Even earlier, at the Cairo summit in 1943, United States president Franklin Roosevelt had discussed the annexation of Tonkin by Chiang Kai-shek's armies.) At the Potsdam Conference it had been decided that Vietnam would first be divided in half; British troops would occupy the south while Chiang's forces occupied the north. French troops would eventually return to Vietnam, and take charge of both sectors. France was intended once more to be Vietnam's colonial master.

For Ho and the Vietnamese people this decision was disastrous. The Vietnamese had neither a voice in the negotiations nor the power to resist the actions of the nations involved. Ho wanted to propose

Admiral Georges Thiérry d'Argenlieu in 1947. After Ho signed a *modus vivendi*, or interim agreement, with Jean Sainteny, allowing the Vietminh government to co-exist with French occupiers, Thiérry d'Argenlieu seized Cochin China, attacking what he called "the anarchy of native revolution."

Ho Chi Minh in 1954 after the French defeat at Dien Bien Phu and the Geneva Conference Agreements. Nine years earlier, before these accords divided Ho's nation into North and South Vietnam, Chinese Guomindang and British troops occupied the country to assist in restoring French colonial rule.

a settlement that would stop the Chinese from entering the country. The Chinese were considered notorious for their cruelty toward conquered peoples. But the Allied powers saw no further need for discussion. To them, the French had every right to resume control of their former colony — even if by force.

It is possible that because Ho's forces were strongest in the north of Vietnam the Chinese were specifically sent there. The French may have hoped that the Vietnamese would eventually beg the French to protect them from the atrocities committed by the Chinese troops. In the meantime, the French forces could grow stronger and in time be able to retake the north from the Chinese.

Ho decided to put into action his wartime blueprint for a governmental takeover. The Vietminh raced to create a provisional government before the catastrophic occupation and partitioning of Vietnam was accomplished. In two weeks time in August 1945 — five days after Japan's surrender — the Vietminh raided Hanoi, then defenseless, and, after very little shooting, the city was theirs.

On August 25, Emperor Bao Dai abdicated his throne and handed the government over to the Vietminh. Ho declared himself president of a provisional government, thereafter to be known as the Democratic Republic of Vietnam. A respected nationalist, Nguyen Hai Than, was appointed vice-president. But soon the foreign troops called for by the Potsdam Agreement began to arrive. In September the British entered Saigon; the Chinese marched into Hanoi, seizing Japanese stragglers who remained.

From the the outset, Vietminh forces were not as successful in establishing themselves in the south. The French maintained a strength and influence in Cochin China they lacked elsewhere in the country. General Douglas Gracey of the British expeditionary force, a staunch supporter of French colonial policy, had begun to disarm Vietnamese nationalist groups, including the Vietminh.

The communists lost their hold in the cities in the south, and were scattered in the countryside. By October, French troops had begun to arrive and

I am a revolutionary. I was born at a time when my country was already a slave state. From the days of my youth I have fought to free it. That is my one merit. In consideration of my past, my companions have voted me head of the government.

—HO CHI MINH
after being named
president of the Democratic
Republic of Vietnam in
August 1945

From left to right: the "Big Three," British Prime Minister Winston Churchill, United States President Harry S. Truman, and Soviet Premier Joseph Stalin attend the Potsdam Conference in 1945. With World War II drawing to a close as Japan neared defeat, the Allied powers agreed to reestablish French Indochina.

were dispatched to the villages to quiet rebellious elements there. Asian history scholar William J. Duicker notes the importance of these developments that occurred 16 years before the United States committed troops to the region: "In effect, within three months of the end of the war, Vietnam had been divided into two hostile zones — a Communist north and a French south. The ultimate

Jean Sainteny (third from left) in Hanoi in 1954. As French emissary to post-World War II Vietnam, Sainteny sought out the politically strongest group in Vietnam to inform them of Allied plans to reoccupy the country. Negotiating with Sainteny, Ho agreed in March 1946 to a Vietminh "free state" within a planned "French Union."

shape of a generation of conflict had begun to take form."

The French sent Jean Sainteny as a representative to whichever Vietnamese group held the most power so that he could explain the decisions reached at the Potsdam Conference. By this time, thousands of people had joined the Vietminh, and the group had many other supporters. Yet the French had no idea who "Ho" was when they sent Sainteny to meet him. Ho met with Sainteny in August 1945, but ignored the official statement from France. Less than a week after the meeting, on September 2, Ho made a speech over the radio to his people. His address was nothing less than a national declaration of independence. Many of the concepts it contained were fashioned after Western political traditions. Ho's speech borrowed freely from the United States' Declaration of Independence, the French Declaration of the Rights of Man, and the writings of the 18th-century revolutionary Thomas Paine.

Ho's point was simple. His people would not easily return to being treated like slaves by the French. They would fight — as the Americans and the French had fought — for the freedom to determine their own political course and national way of life.

In his radio declaration, Ho accused the French of denying the Vietnamese people their essential dignity as human beings, and of refusing to recognize their equal right to basic human freedoms. What had once been part of three constituent regions of French Indochina was now the Democratic Republic of Vietnam. He added that he was actually taking over the government from the Japanese since, he explained, the French had given up their rule during World War II. "Since the autumn of 1940 our country has ceased to be a colony and had become a Japanese outpost. . . . We have wrested our independence from the Japanese and not the French. The French have fled, the Japanese have capitulated, Emperor Bao Dai has abdicated, our people have broken down the fetters which for over a century have tied us down; our people have at the same time overthrown the monarchic constitution that had reigned supreme for so many centuries and instead have established the present Republican government."

Mixed with his words of patriotism were actions of deceit and violence. Ho ordered his military specialist Giap to have all opposing Vietnamese leaders killed, as well as anyone else who spoke out against Ho or the Vietminh. Ho attended all the funerals, but he never showed any remorse for those he believed had stood in the way of his leadership and of communism.

> *It was the determination of Ho, his colleagues and successors, to dominate the entire country, including Laos and Cambodia, which was, from 1945 onwards, the principal dynamic of the struggle and the ultimate cause of all the bloodshed. America's errors were merely a contributory factor.*
> —PAUL JOHNSON
> British historian

Though he knew that the French were planning to return, Ho began to put together a governing cabinet. This group of men would gather information for him and serve as his counselors. Ho chose young, inexperienced people who could be influenced easily and who were unlikely to challenge him on major national issues and strategies. Ho Chi Minh wanted final decision-making power to rest personally with him.

Although Ho was a national hero by this time, few people knew even what he looked like. Those who encountered their new leader were surprised to find him wearing shorts, a colonial helmet, and carrying a walking stick. He looked as if he had been working in a rice paddy all his life, and this pleased the Vietnamese.

Relations between the French and the Vietnamese people grew increasingly troubled. The colonial French population persisted in regarding the Vietnamese as little more than children to be supervised. Colonists tried to torpedo any negotiations between Ho and the French government before they were underway. To them, all that was necessary was to restore French Indochina. They were completely blind to the changes that had occurred among the Vietnamese people during the past two decades.

Ho held intensive talks with French negotiator Jean Sainteny as pressure to reach an agreement was growing. But negotiations were going poorly, and in March 1946, with French troops sailing toward Vietnam, war seemed imminent. Finally, Ho agreed to an accord on March 6 through which France recognized the Democratic Republic of Vietnam as a "free state," with its own "government, parliament . . . and treasury" — but as part of the so-called French Union. This agreement allowed French military personnel to remain, ostensibly in order to relieve the Chinese occupation troops and to eliminate any lingering Japanese troops. Of course there was no serious intent on the part of France to remove its soldiers. Both sides agreed to open further negotiations soon to work out the exact details. When Sainteny told Ho how pleased he was with the agreement, Ho answered, "I'm not so

Taxes, forced labor, exploitation, that is the summing up of your civilization.

—HO CHI MINH
on French society

84

pleased, for really it is you who have benefited; you know perfectly well I wanted more than this. . . . Still, one can't have everything overnight."

Ho had successfully bought time for his people. Until this agreement was dissolved, the Vietminh was able to prepare for the war for independence.

As popular as Ho was, upon hearing the terms of this *modus vivendi* (interim agreement) scores of Vietnamese became irate. They felt he had betrayed

A French Foreign legionnaire guards a captured Vietminh guerrilla while another examines a Vietminh flag bearing the communist hammer and sickle. Ho's military commander, Giap, discovered that such lightly equipped troops could wage an effective guerrilla war against the less mobile, heavily equipped French.

85

them. To allay these feelings of anger and suspicion, Ho addressed a large rally, and, with tears in his eyes, explained: "I, Ho Chi Minh, have always sent you along the path to freedom; I have spent my whole life fighting for our country's independence. You know I would sooner die than betray the nation. I swear I have not betrayed you."

The French troops arrived and more colonists soon followed. The French colonists still insisted on their superiority to the Vietnamese. They also feared and hated communism. One French admiral, Georges Thiérry d'Argenlieu, openly argued for "France's greatness, that would not permit the anarchy of native revolution." He was prominent among those Frenchmen who did not wish for peace between the French and Vietnamese, but for war, and the chance to destroy the Vietminh. When Ho was asked by a Western journalist about his chances of defeating the French troops, he responded with an allegory: "We will be like the elephant and the tiger. When the elephant is strong and rested and near his base we will retreat. And if the tiger ever pauses the elephant will impale him on his mighty tusks. But the tiger will not pause and the elephant will die of exhaustion and loss of blood."

There was short-term peace in the north under General Jacques Leclerc. However, in the south relations were strained between the French and Vietnamese. Admiral d'Argenlieu had been assigned there. In the small town of Dalat, d'Argenlieu schemed to make Cochin China into a separate government — that answered only to Paris.

D'Argenlieu waited until Ho was in France, ratifying the agreement signed in Vietnam, to proclaim the Cochin China area as a separate republic. This area was culturally and historically no less a part of Vietnam than Annam or Tonkin. Its excellent rice production and its large-scale rubber plantations provided food and export income precious to French financial interests.

Ho and his advisers were stunned when they learned about losing Cochin China, but chose to ignore the problem temporarily. They were still in France and needed to ratify the latest treaty. Ho was

> *Why do they rule the world,*
> *While we bow our heads*
> *as slaves?*
> —from an anonymous
> Vietnamese nationalist poem

welcomed as a celebrity in Paris. In 1919 he had sat in a basement and waited to be called to meet Woodrow Wilson — a call that never came. By 1946 he was being photographed with French statesmen and diplomats as the Vietnamese head of state.

When d'Argenlieu took over Cochin China, Ho Chi Minh's attempts to negotiate in France were hobbled. The hero of the Free French military effort against the Germans during World War II, the conservative general Charles de Gaulle, was gaining

As president of the Democratic Republic of Vietnam, Ho signs the guest book at city hall in Paris in 1946, where 27 years earlier he had been an obscure Vietnamese nationalist and radical. While Ho negotiated unsuccessfully for Vietnam's independence, armed clashes occurred between French colonists and Vietnamese.

AP/WIDE WORLD

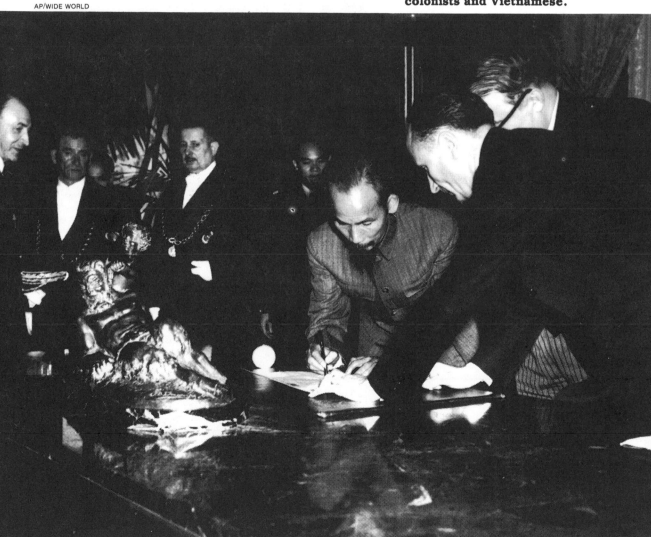

A photograph from December 1950 shows Ho Chi Minh at age 60. Earlier this same year, the People's Republic of China, led by Chairman Mao Zedong, became the first country to recognize the Democratic Republic of Vietnam. The Soviet Union was the second nation to recognize Ho's government.

UPI/BETTMANN NEWSPHOTOS

enormous political support in France. A party built around de Gaulle's leadership called on France to rebuild its greatness as a world power. In Fontaine-bleau, Ho met with French delegates who were decisively against independence for Vietnam. Instead Ho signed a preliminary agreement in September 1946 to meet again on the matter in the future; this agreement also provided for a cease-fire. There were now brutal confrontations taking place between Vietnamese and French soldiers.

Relations between the French and the Vietnamese continued to deteriorate. In November the French attempted to open a customs house in the Tonkin port of Haiphong in order to collect import and export taxes. The Vietminh protested vehemently and the French sent in naval and infantry forces. The incident climaxed with the French ship *Suffren* shelling the harbor, killing thousands of civilians. At almost the same time the first president of the Republic of Cochin China, Nguyen Van Trinh, appointed by the French, hanged himself.

Ho Chi Minh embraces Marshal Josip Broz Tito, Yugoslavia's communist president, in Belgrade, the nation's capital. While Ho organized the Vietminh to take power after the Japanese met defeat in World War II, Tito led his partisan guerrillas against German forces in Yugoslavia. Both leaders' names were aliases.

A United States marine orders North Korean prisoners to keep their hands high. When North Korean and Chinese communist troops invaded noncommunist South Korea in 1950, the United States entered the Korean War and increased aid to French forces fighting Ho's government in Vietnam.

Both France and Ho Chi Minh attempted to stop the fighting, but d'Argenlieu kept interfering and prolonging the battle. The French again sent Sainteny as a representative to talk with Ho, but the admiral delayed Sainteny's arrival for 10 days. Ho wrote to the socialist Léon Blum, who was serving as French premier during December 1946, but d'Argenlieu made certain to intercept the letters. Ho continued to send messages unaware that they were never delivered.

Since neither side was able to communicate with

UPI/BETTMANN NEWSPHOTOS

the other, open war was soon to erupt. On December 19, 1946, Ho called on the people to commence active resistance against the French. The following day, Ho and Giap were surrounded in the president's headquarters by French troops and had to flee under a hail of bullets to the rice paddies outside Hanoi. The following day Ho made a radio address, directed to the nations of the world. He stated that he felt betrayed by the agreement that had been reached earlier, and felt that international laws were only made for weaker nations to follow. The stronger nations appeared to do as they pleased.

Ho blamed the French colonials and Admiral d'Argenlieu — not France — for starting the war. He asked the French soldiers to lay down their weapons to avoid a dishonorable conflict. He also told his forces to defend themselves and retaliate when attacked, and to remain dedicated to the cause of national freedom: "Our resistance will be long and painful, but whatever the sacrifices, however long the struggle, we shall fight to the end, until Vietnam is fully independent and reunified."

After leaving Giap to oversee most of the fighting, Ho settled in a town 60 miles northwest of Hanoi to concentrate on negotiations with the French.

In the meantime, the French had brought the former emperor, Bao Dai, out of exile in Hong Kong and installed him as the puppet ruler of Vietnam. Talks with the French concerning Bao Dai becoming the head of a French-devised "Associated State of Vietnam" had started in 1945. In 1949 the former emperor gave in to the "Bao Dai Solution." In the meantime, the Chinese civil war between Mao Zedong's communists and Chiang's Guomindang nationalists broke out. Although in the midst of a long, bloody struggle, Mao recognized Ho Chi Minh as the official head of Vietnam and gave him supplies and weapons to fight the French. Later the Soviet Union also supplied Ho with weapons. The Soviet satellite countries, such as Romania, Poland, Hungary, Czechoslovakia, and East Germany, also recognized Ho as leader. The French were now dealing with more than a mere rebel agitator.

Ho was given weapons and credit for more pur-

> *How funny life is! When I was in prison in China, there were always two armed guards standing right over me with guns. Now I'm president of the Vietnam Republic, and whenever I leave [government headquarters] there are two armed guards right over me, with their guns.*
> —HO CHI MINH

chases, and had millions of communist supporters. He did not, however, openly declare his communist beliefs. In fact, he had already dissolved the Indochinese Communist party in 1945, renaming the organization the *Lien Viet*, or Vietnamese Alliance, which tried to take a middle-of-the-road position between extremes in political ideology. In the early 1950s, however, Ho himself warned against such moderate positions, saying, "There are two chairs. You are invited to sit on whichever you like, but please don't sit between the two for you risk falling down when the chairs move apart."

> *The loss of South Vietnam would set in motion a crumbling process that could, as it progressed, have grave consequences for us and for freedom.*
> —DWIGHT D. EISENHOWER
> American president
> (1953–61)

The French used this connection to the communists to work against Ho. By claiming he was a communist, the French were able to get arms from the United States, which was becoming more and more hostile toward communist nations, especially the Soviet Union. As tension built, the United States and the Soviet Union began to engage in a complex political and economic conflict called the Cold War. An almost hysterical fear of communism characterized both America's domestic scene and its foreign policy during the 1950s. To prevent the spread of communism in Southeast Asia, the United States immediately gave France the support it asked for.

Ho attempted to show that Vietnam represented many political beliefs, but the Western powers really didn't believe his claims.

The lack of Western political support meant little to the people of Vietnam; they would go to any lengths to achieve their freedom. Since 1947 the Vietminh were in a struggle for survival in the Viet Bac mountains, the Central Highlands, and the Plain of Reeds. And with each bomb dropped, with each military assault, Ho received more enthusiastic recruits. Though the French had a clear military superiority, the Vietminh had on their side something far more important — the hearts and minds of the people.

In 1950 the Korean War erupted. The Chinese communists hurled their Red Army across the border into Korea to assist the spread of communism there. The United States, as part of a United Nations expedition, fought against the Chinese and Korean communist forces, while continuing to send aid to the French so that they might crush the Vietminh. Eventually, due to pressure in his own government, Ho declared his belief in communism.

For the people of France, the question of what to do in Southeast Asia was proving increasingly difficult. Many of the French did not want to fight to retain Vietnam. The colonial era was over, but the French had not yet learned this painful lesson.

The head of the Catholic church in Ninh Binh province talks with a fighter from the North Vietnamese People's Volunteer Corps in 1967 — the height of the Vietnam War. When Vietnam was divided in 1954 into Ho's northern Democratic Republic of Vietnam and the pro-Western government in the south, about 800,000 Catholics fled the north.

GIRAUDON/ART RESOURCE

7

To Battle Giants

The French occupation of Vietnam ended with the battle at Dien Bien Phu in 1954. The fighting there resulted in an extraordinary victory for General Vo Nguyen Giap and the Vietminh.

But the years intervening between 1945 and this surprising final defeat for the French were extremely difficult ones for Ho and his fledgling government. During this period, Mao Zedong's Red Army was trying to outmaneuver Chiang Kai-shek's nationalist troops in the bitter civil war then raging in China. The embattled Chinese communists were unable to help their Vietnamese counterparts in their struggle to prevent the French from reimposing colonial rule in Vietnam. At about this time Giap commented: "The revolutionary leader must find out the general and particular laws of events in a maze of phenomena in which the false is hardly distinguishable from the true."

Ho's Vietminh had weathered the previous year's hardships in the mountains, and, by 1948, their recruits had increased sufficiently to nearly equal the once much larger French army. Although the Vietminh was still not well enough equipped to put

AP/WIDE WORLD

French General Henri Navarre with his officers. Navarre felt assured of a quick and decisive victory over the Vietminh at Dien Bien Phu. The French planned to cut off Vietminh supply lines and stop future communist offensives. The French, however, found themselves ambushed by Giap's guerrillas, and were routed. Negotiations with Ho's government began the next day.

Ho Chi Minh in 1969 Although the Vietminh victory at Dien Bien Phu enabled Ho's government to gain independence for North Vietnam, the United States, which considered Ho an aggressor, objected to the Geneva accords, and helped install Ngo Dinh Diem's regime in the southern part of Vietnam.

EASTFOTO

the French at a serious disadvantage, it was clear that the Europeans did not want to fight a long, bloody conflict. The return of Bao Dai to the throne in 1949 had also been somewhat damaging to Ho's aim to represent the Vietnamese desire for independence. With the emperor seeming to lead a French-created "State of Vietnam," Ho Chi Minh appeared to some — such as United States Secretary of State Dean Acheson — to be attacking a legitimate Vietnamese regime. Yet the slogan used by Ho to remind the Vietnamese of the need for national unity was "Fatherland above all."

Mao and the Red Army succeeded in driving Chiang's armies out of mainland China in the fall of 1949. Early in 1950 Vo Nguyen Giap went on a diplomatic mission to ask the People's Republic of China, formed under Mao, for military assistance. Before long, Ho was able to sign an agreement for arms from the Chinese. Ho's Democratic Republic of Vietnam, or the DRV, also received official Chinese recognition as Vietnam's only legitimate government. Soviet approval of Ho's government followed shortly thereafter. French military expenditures by this stage had grown to more than half the amount allocated for purposes of fighting to regain the colony.

However, in February the United States announced its recognition of the Bao Dai government, which was powerless except as an extension of French policies. That same year, with Harry Truman as president, the United States took the first step toward what would become years of intense involvement in Southeast Asia, with far-ranging consequences: Washington began sending military aid to the French, totaling $3.6 billion by 1954. A country that had been merely one part of French Indochina was fast becoming a focal point of Chinese and United States foreign policy — not only that of the French.

With China making military equipment available to the Vietnamese communists, Giap's soldiers were emboldened. He initiated an attack in 1950 against French garrisons along the Red River delta south of Hanoi. But the French command had also tough-

> *As for those who continue to adopt a "middle-of-the-road" attitude, let me urge them to make a quick and definite choice: the fatherland or the enemy.*
>
> —HO CHI MINH

ened, and the Vietminh were thrown back. The quality of French military leadership against Ho was probably at its peak under General Jean-Marie-Gabriel de Lattre de Tassigny, who used aircraft against the advancing enemy.

In response, the communists chose to rely on ambushes and guerrilla tactics instead of direct confrontation. The Vietminh could not do battle with the French using conventional means. Their change in strategy began to take a toll on the French armed forces and French public opinion began to take a more critical tone toward the war in Indochina. France had resisted reaching a peaceful settlement to the clash with Ho Chi Minh's DRV. As long as

An official confers with landowners in the southern Republic of Vietnam (RVN) concerning the Diem government's land reform program in 1957. Before the 1954 Geneva Conference Agreements, land had been redistributed to peasants in Vietminh-controlled areas at no cost or at reduced rents. Diem sought to undo these policies.

Ngo Dinh Diem received United States support shortly after the Geneva Conference and was appointed prime minister of South Vietnam by Emperor Bao Dai in 1954, whom Diem deposed in 1955. Diem persecuted remnants of the Vietminh in the south, and later arrested, imprisoned, and executed citizens he considered dangerous to his rule. He was assassinated in 1963.

the DRV existed the French could not reassert colonial supremacy in the area. Since conquest was the ultimate French objective, the Vietminh had no choice but to keep fighting or surrender their goal of self-determination.

Ho had repeatedly urged France to avoid war as a solution to the question of Vietnamese independence. As the war continued, and its cost mounted, there seemed little promise of victory for either side. France slowly came around to viewing the negotiating table, rather than the battlefield, as a way to solve the dispute. However, it was the unexpected and humiliating defeat at Dien Bien Phu that finally persuaded the French to go to Geneva, Switzerland, to negotiate.

At Dien Bien Phu the French commander, General Henri Navarre, was expecting a great victory over the Vietminh. He had positioned his troops in a valley surrounded by towering cliffs. Navarre wanted to lure the Vietnamese into the valley, pin them down, and massacre them there. Surrounded by the nearly impassable mountains, this position seemed secure. But Navarre lacked certain vital information about the enemy; he was unaware of Giap's military abilities and the dedication of the Vietminh troops. The Vietminh soldiers, heading to the battlegrounds, dismantled their heavy artillery and, piece by piece, strapped the machinery to their backs. Like a train of mules, they crossed the mountains, climbed steep inclines during monsoon rains and in the dark of night. In this way they carried heavy weaponry, one disassembled part following another, until they reached the battle site. Once in position, they reassembled the artillery and set in motion one of their most devastating attacks.

While the French crouched in their trenches, they found themselves suddenly in the midst of a Vietminh ambush. The very next day, May 8, 1950, Ho arranged to meet the French in Geneva, to negotiate a cease-fire. Foreign Minister Pham Van Dong had the responsibility of following up Giap's military accomplishments at the talks. Ho had finally achieved the strength necessary to bargain with a major Western power. But the United States would not let the French military defeat turn into a rout of the Western military and political presence in Asia.

Richard Nixon (then vice-president under Dwight D. Eisenhower) stated that if South Vietnam was taken by the communists, other countries in Southeast Asia would fall one by one to communism like a row of toppling dominoes; the United States was determined not to let this happen.

Pham Van Dong as prime minister of the Democratic Republic of Vietnam. Pham participated in the short-lived Student's movement against French colonialism, and met Ho in Canton, China, in 1925. In 1930 he marched with peasants on the town of Vinh. As Ho's foreign minister, he negotiated with the French at the Geneva Conference in 1954.

EASTFOTO

A guerrilla soldier of the National Liberation Front aims his rocket launcher. Resistance groups in the south, called the Viet Cong by the United States and South Vietnamese governments, formed the NLF in December 1961. During the Vietnam War, NLF forces spearheaded the Tet offensive in 1968 against the south.

It was Pham Van Dong's task to convey to Ho Chi Minh the Soviet Union's stern warning that if the United States became involved in Vietnam, China might also enter the arena. The Soviets were concerned that China's joining the conflict would make it global in scale. To prevent this, Ho's allies in China and the Soviet Union took his victory away from him. They indicated to the French that a united Vietnam would not be in the Soviet interest. Historian Gabriel Kalko notes that "the Chinese and the Russians were much closer to each other than . . . they were to the Vietnamese Communists." Though Ho held most of Vietnam, he was strongly advised to relinquish the south. Ho's wait for a united independent Vietnam was to be prolonged. He would not live to see his nation unified by the north's victory over the south 21 years later.

The Geneva Conference Agreements signed in July 1954 divided Vietnam into two zones at the

17th Parallel. The north was subsequently urged by the Chinese and Soviets to respect this boundary. These agreements met instantly with disapproval from the United States, which demanded that Vietnam be unified in accordance with the outcome of elections that it would oversee. Through the Geneva agreement Ho and his forces were limited to the northern half of Annam and the province of Tonkin, while the United States government undertook to reorganize Cochin China and the southern half of Annam. The entire Vietnamese population, as the agreements stipulated, would vote in a national election within two years to decide the fate of both zones. A delegation from the United States had attended the Geneva Conference and found the division (which later led to the region being referred to as North and South Vietnam) barely acceptable. Secretary of State John Foster Dulles had wanted to convince France and Great Britain that, by joining forces with the United States, Ho's regime could be destroyed.

An International Commission, with representatives from Canada, Poland, and India, was established in Vietnam to report on violations of the Geneva Conference Agreements. It protested the fact that the national elections called for under the agreements were never held. The United States had refused to sign the agreements, and therefore had removed itself from the international rules established under them. According to the United States' Central Intelligence Agency, if the national elections had been in 1956, as planned, Ho Chi Minh would "almost certainly" have won. As a result, the commission's report was ignored, and the United States continued to dominate the south.

Prospects of renewed foreign intervention were a significant problem for Ho, but there were more pressing problems within his nation. Famine had become widespread throughout the Democratic Republic of Vietnam. In an attempt both to remedy this disaster, and to start a domestic policy in line with communist practices elsewhere, Ho began a new farm program in this same year. It was modeled after similar programs launched in China by Mao

When we marched into the rice paddies we carried, along with our packs and our rifles, the implicit convictions that the Viet Cong could be quickly beaten. We kept the packs and rifles; the convictions, we lost.
—PHILIP CAPUTO
American journalist and soldier in Vietnam

Le Duan, the Democratic Republic of Vietnam's general secretary of the Vietnamese Communist party. Le Duan, often considered Ho's second in command, was responsible for representing the communist resistance organizations in the south before the DRV's leadership.

Zedong. Farmers were to give up their small plots and work instead on large government-owned farms. Peasants were so angered by the government's attempt to overhaul land ownership and farming methods, they put up resistance. Armed suppression of ensuing uprisings may have cost tens of thousands of lives. Some sources estimate that perhaps as many as 100,000 peasants were executed. A rebellion broke out in the province of Nghe An, where Ho himself had been born, and where the first *Xo Viets,* or village councils, had sprung up in the 1930s. Two years later, Ho asked that the north-south border be opened for trade, since the south grew most of the rice in Vietnam. The north badly needed more rice to feed its people. But the southern leader, Ngo Dinh Diem, refused to trade with the north. Having been appointed prime minister in the summer of 1954 with help from the United States, Diem had deposed Bao Dai the next year by calling a special election. He had also been given more than $300 million in U.S. aid the year following the Geneva Conference.

Diem also reversed certain reforms made previous to the conference in Vietminh-governed pockets in the south. Land had been wrested from the landlords and allocated to peasant farmers. Diem's attempts at land reform — conducted with United States support — caused peasants to pay for land the Vietminh had already distributed to them at no cost or at reduced rents. Returning landlords also took back their lands. It is estimated that 50 percent of the farmland was owned by two and one-half percent of the landowners.

Diem's abuses of power helped bring the United States into an eventual confrontation with Ho and the Democratic Republic of Vietnam. Diem openly persecuted former members of the Vietminh. About 15,000 original members still remained in the south by 1957. Since the southern Republic of Vietnam treated these men as the enemy, they began to form small detachments that would harass and sabotage Diem's forces. These groups were referred to by Diem himself as the *Viet Cong.* Although the United States claimed for many years that Ho was simply sending guerrillas south, these rebels, in most cases, were actually southern citizens fighting against a corrupt regime. Already authorized to have arrested and imprisoned anyone thought to be subversive or dangerous to his rule, Diem introduced Law 10/59 in 1959. This law made it legal for him to execute citizens without a trial or other procedure. Now Diem was censoring the press and arresting scores of people, charging them with political crimes. (By 1960, there were nearly 50,000 political prisoners in the south.)

Ho had known of Diem since 1945. When hostilities with the French resumed after World War II, Ho had asked Diem to help the Vietminh. The politician turned down the request. Diem, a Catholic

President of the United States from 1961 until his assassination in 1963, John F. Kennedy talks with General William Yarborough. The Kennedy administration's "graduated response" to the National Liberation Front's war against Ngo Dinh Diem's regime brought the number of U.S. troops in South Vietnam to 3,200 by 1961.

who also held Confucian ideas in high regard, was an anticommunist. About 800,000 Catholics had fled the north after the Geneva Conference Agreements. This increased their numbers in the south to approximately 2 million, and Diem depended on this large Catholic constituency.

Ho made the unification of North and South Vietnam his top priority. His first step was to appoint Le Duan, a communist leader from the south, as his party secretary in the north. Le Duan made the southern resistance movement a crucial issue before the Vietminh leadership. In December 1960, a formal organization was created from the Viet Cong organizations. This was known as the National Liberation Front, or NLF.

Now that the communist-controlled Vietminh openly supported the National Liberation Front, the United States stepped up its assistance to the Diem regime. President John F. Kennedy sent personnel as well as arms, and by late 1961 there were 3,200 United States troops in the area. Pham Van Dong remarked, "Diem is unpopular and the more unpopular he is, the more American aid he will need to remain in power. And the more American aid he gets, the more of an American puppet he'll look and the less likely he is to regain popularity. . . . It is a downward spiral."

On May 8, 1963, nine Vietnamese Buddhists were killed by Diem's troops during a demonstration against the South Vietnamese premier. Briefly, Diem's repression of the Buddhists caused disaffection with him in the United States government, which responded by cutting aid to the south. From 1963 until 1967, the Buddhists continued to protest, notably in the cities of Hué and Da Nang, as United States troop involvement expanded in the war between the two Vietnams. South Vietnamese generals were advised by United States officials to force Diem from office. Six months after the Buddhists were killed, Diem and his brother were assassinated in a military takeover. American aid was quickly restored. Diem's death resulted in chaos for South Vietnam. The nation saw a scramble for power as eight governments rose and fell in less

UPI/BETTMANN NEWSPHOTOS

Following Diem's assassination Air Marshal Nguyen Cao Ky became head of state in South Vietnam in 1965 after eight separate regimes rose and fell in 18 months. General Nguyen Van Thieu became president and Ky his vice-president in national elections two years later.

than 18 months before Air Marshal Nguyen Cao Ky finally became president, with General Nguyen Van Thieu as vice-president. (In 1967 Thieu would be elected president.) South Vietnam's armed forces, meanwhile, had begun losing the will to fight the National Liberation Front. While the government there had been in a state of turmoil, its troops lost morale and often collaborated with the enemy. Nevertheless, the United States supported the Republic of Vietnam, thoroughly convinced that only the defense of the south stood between the rest of Southeast Asia and communism.

The Viet Cong and the United States-supported Army of the Republic of Vietnam (ARVN) differed from one another socially and economically. The Viet Cong consisted primarily of peasants who had grown up in poverty and without any formal education. They had fought against the French colonials and believed that victory was their only hope

United States Vice-President Lyndon Baines Johnson on a visit to South Vietnam. He holds the South Vietnamese flag as his motorcade proceeds to the capital, Saigon. Following John F. Kennedy's assassination, Johnson succeeded him and subsequently won the 1964 presidential election. Johnson's escalation of the war against Ho's government ruined his chances for reelection.

AP/WIDE WORLD

for a better future. The ARVN's soldiers had come largely from urban, frequently upper-class, families who had prospered under French rule. Unlike the Viet Cong, they had little or no support among the peasants.

The Viet Cong's tactics were especially designed for warfare in Vietnam's jungle terrain. The ARVN deployed its troops in a conventional manner, confined its activities to daylight hours, and made its headquarters in cities. Later, the ARVN became increasingly dependent on United States air support.

Lyndon Baines Johnson, who had been sworn in as president following John F. Kennedy's assassination in November 1963, insisted that the United States continue the fight. His advisers were excessively optimistic, too proud to retreat, and convinced that their technologically superior military could overwhelm the Viet Cong. Johnson gradually built up troop levels and began to use aircraft such

Outside the city of Da Nang, South Vietnamese villagers huddle beside a mother and child killed in a napalm strike. Another woman holds her seriously burned daughter. A jellied gasoline compound, napalm was used in U.S. and South Vietnamese air strikes against suspected Viet Cong strongholds.

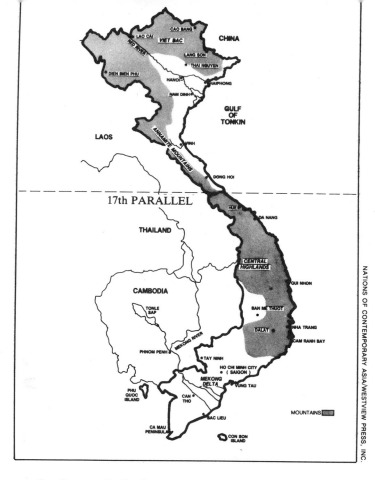

NATIONS OF CONTEMPORARY ASIA/WESTVIEW PRESS, INC.

This map shows Vietnam at the conclusion of the Vietnam War. The 17th Parallel, shown here, was established by the Geneva Conference Agreements in July 1954, dividing the nation into North and South Vietnam. Once reunified by communist forces in 1975, the nation was called the Socialist Republic of Vietnam.

as the heavy B-52 bomber to devastate targets inside Vietnam. This process came to be called "graduated response." Bombing was used unsuccessfully throughout the war to destroy the Ho Chi Minh Trail, along which supplies and munitions flowed to the NLF in the south.

Congress made a decision in August 1964 that irreversibly changed the nature of the war. It passed the Gulf of Tonkin Resolution, which cleared the way for the United States to intervene with armed might directly, anywhere in Southeast Asia. This resolution was prepared in advance of the incident that triggered its approval. An invasion by Ho of the south was considered imminent. An American vessel, carrying intelligence-gathering equipment, was sent into North Vietnamese coastal waters. The spy ship was soon attacked by gunboats, when it was concluded that the ship was on an espionage mission. Having successfully provoked the Democratic

Republic of Vietnam to respond militarily against its forces, the United States could then use the incident to justify more military operations.

Ho was, in fact, tired of war and tried many times to meet with United States representatives to negotiate an end to the conflict. In 1964 he sent word to the secretary-general of the United Nations that he would meet with the American negotiators under any conditions. The United States not only ignored the offer, it kept the proposal a secret. Ho made six more offers to seek a peaceful settlement before his efforts toward a diplomatic accord were publicly known. The peace proposals were rejected because officials in the Johnson administration denied that Ho was serious about such a settlement. Secretary of Defense Robert McNamara opposed holding talks because he wanted a settlement that would punish Ho Chi Minh. Rational concerns were sacrificed as thousands died on both sides.

The United States published a report in February 1965, defending its active role in the Vietnam War. The report placed the blame for the war's continuance on Ho Chi Minh in Hanoi, stating that the Democratic Republic of Vietnam was the aggressor and was deliberately prolonging the war. As early as the Geneva Conference, Ho Chi Minh had been called aggressive by American officials such as John Foster Dulles, who had hoped that the Vietminh representatives had come to the conference to "purge themselves of their aggression."

Ho replied to the report's charges: If President Johnson wanted to unite Vietnam, all he had to do was adhere to the Geneva Agreements and remove the American troops.

President Johnson, confident that victory was near, regarded Ho's suggestion as out of the question, and ordered the bombing of cities in the north. The devastation continued. Vietnamese civilians were in the midst of war's mayhem. Villages were flattened; communities were terrorized. Advanced American military technology, such as helicopter gunships, napalm, and aerial bombing, disrupted Vietnamese peasant life in the south, often bringing injury and death to civilians. Southern peasants

Now we have a problem in making our power credible and Vietnam looks like the place.
—JOHN F. KENNEDY
American president (1960–63), shortly after the failure of the U.S.-backed invasion of communist Cuba in 1961

who had become refugees — about 720,000 in 1964 alone — did so at various times to escape the immense firepower brought into action by the ARVN and the United States forces.

Ho approached the French in an attempt to bring peace to his nation. He spoke again with the French representative Jean Sainteny, and said that his only demand was that foreign troops withdraw. The Americans responded by saying that Ho must first remove his own forces and supporters in the south. Ho could not comply, however. It was claimed he controlled the southern group, the National Liberation Front, but by this time the NLF was operating on its own initiative.

Ho sought to persuade world opinion that the United States' activities were misguided, unjust, and immoral. He brought reporters to locations in North Vietnam where American bombers had demolished villages — waging war on the population itself. The principles for which those forces

Demonstrators release symbolic black and white balloons in New York City's Central Park in 1969 to protest United States military activity in Vietnam. The number of U.S. troops in Vietnam climbed to 532,400 that year. Increasing numbers of young Americans demanded an end to U.S. involvement in Vietnam, while many young men fled the country to escape military service as the war escalated.

AP/WIDE WORLD

South Vietnamese president Nguyen Van Thieu with President Richard M. Nixon of the United States in June 1969. Nixon met with Thieu to discuss reducing U.S. military forces in South Vietnam. Nixon's program of gradual troop withdrawal came to be called "Vietnamization."

UPI/BETTMANN NEWSPHOTOS

were fighting proved increasingly muddled and illogical. After the savage NLF Tet offensive (named for the Vietnamese New Year) in January and February 1968, an American officer commented about the village of Ben Tre: "We had to destroy the town to save it." Ho told the press the Vietnamese were given only two choices: slavery to the United States or victory. "We have no alternative," he said.

American public opinion was becoming disillusioned with the war. An emerging majority of Americans became steadily less concerned with the war's outcome than with seeing it end. At home, young men began to avoid the draft by fleeing the country. Mass rallies were held in the nation's capital, major cities, and on university campuses, fervently protesting United States participation in the war.

By the time of the 1968 presidential elections, Johnson chose not to run, aware that he would not be reelected under the circumstances. The Republican party nominee Richard Nixon won the election against Johnson's former vice-president, Hubert Humphrey, after promising that he could end the war. Nixon's "Vietnamization" program was intended to remove American troops while teaching the South Vietnamese to assume the defense of their nation.

The Paris peace talks began in April of 1969, and the United States began gradually to pull its forces out of Vietnam. The last Americans would leave as the People's Army of Vietnam (PAVN) rumbled into Saigon in April 1975.

Ho did not live to see the war's end. On September 3, 1969, Ho Chi Minh died of a massive heart attack. He had changed the course of history on two entire continents, if not the world. As he said himself in a 1966 radio interview, he had devoted his life to the freedom of his country: "Nothing is more precious than independence and freedom. When victory comes, our people will rebuild our country." On July 2, 1976, the goal to which Ho had dedicated his life's energies was realized: North and South Vietnam were officially reunited as the Socialist Republic of Vietnam. The city of Saigon was renamed Ho Chi Minh City.

Ho Chi Minh lies in state in Hanoi as Vietnamese Communist party secretary Le Duan stands by the casket. The president of the Democratic Republic of Vietnam since 1945, Ho Chi Minh died of a massive heart attack on September 3, 1969. Ho led the communists to victory over French colonialism, but would not live to see North and South Vietnam's unification.

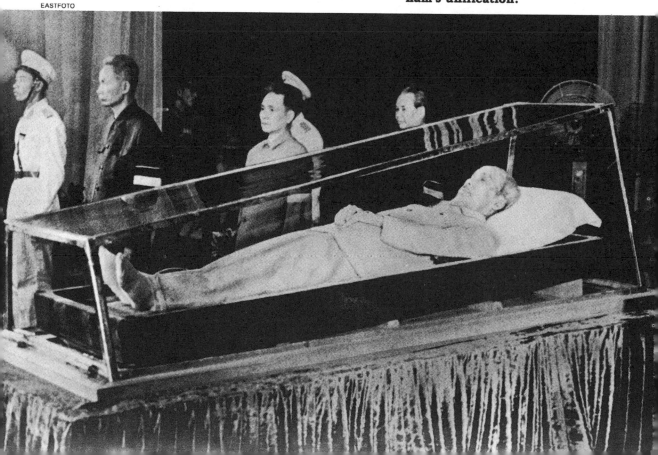

Further Reading

Duncanson, Dennis J. *Government and Revolution in Vietnam.* London: Oxford University Press, 1968.

Fall, Bernard. *Ho Chi Minh on Revolution.* New York: Frederick A. Praeger, 1967.

Fenn, Charles. *Ho Chi Minh.* New York: Charles Scribner's Sons, 1973.

FitzGerald, Frances. *Fire in the Lake.* Boston: Little, Brown and Co., Inc., 1972.

Halberstam, David. *Ho.* New York: Random House, 1971.

Herr, Michael. *Dispatches.* New York: Alfred A. Knopf, Inc., 1977.

Ho Chi Minh. *Prison Diary.* Hanoi: Foreign Languages Publishing House, 1965.

Hoang Van Chi. *From Colonialism to Communism.* New York: Frederick A. Praeger, 1964.

Kolko, Gabriel. *Anatomy of a War.* New York: Pantheon Books, 1985.

Lacouture, Jean. *Vietnam Between Two Truces.* New York: Random House, 1966.

———. *Ho Chi Minh: A Political Biography.* New York: Random House, 1968.

McAlister, John, and Paul Mus. *The Vietnamese and Their Revolution.* New York: Harper & Row, 1970.

Chronology

May 19, 1890	Born Nguyen Sinh Cung in the French protectorate of Annam
1909	Expelled from school for distributing anticolonialist newspapers
1911	Joins crew of French merchant ship; settles in France a few years later
1919	Unsuccessfully attempts to petition for Indochinese independence at the Versailles Peace Conference
1920	Joins French Communist party
1923–24	Visits Moscow; attends the Fifth Congress of the Communist International
1926	Founds the Association of Vietnamese Revolutionary Youth in China
1930	Organizes the Vietnamese Communist party (later the Indochinese Communist party) in Hong Kong
1931–32	Jailed by British in Hong Kong
1940	Germany invades France; Japanese enter Vietnam
1941	Ho returns to Vietnam; founds the Vietminh, a communist independence movement
1942–44	Imprisoned in China
Aug. 1945	The Vietminh seizes power; Emperor Bao Dai abdicates; Ho becomes president of the Democratic Republic of Vietnam
Sept. 1945	Until the French are able to return, Chinese occupy North Vietnam; British occupy South Vietnam
Nov. 1946	French shell northern port city of Haiphong
Dec. 1946	The Vietminh attacks French troops stationed in Hanoi, beginning the Indochina War
1949	France establishes a puppet government under Bao Dai, in opposition to Ho's regime
1954	French defeated at Dien Bien Phu, ending French occupation of Vietnam; Vietnam is split at 17th parallel
1955	Premier Ngo Dinh Diem deposes Emperor Bao Dai
1956	Communist land reforms spark riots in North Vietnam
1960	North Vietnamese-backed National Liberation Front (NLF) created in South Vietnam to oppose Diem's government
1963	Diem assassinated
Aug. 1964	North Vietnam attacks U.S. spy ship in the Gulf of Tonkin; United States attacks North Vietnam's military bases in response
Jan.–Feb. 1968	NLF launches the Tet Offensive in South Vietnam
May 1969	First U.S. troop withdrawal
Sept. 3, 1969	Ho dies of heart attack
July 2, 1976	North and South Vietnam unified as the Socialist Republic of Vietnam

Index

Dana Ohlmeyer Lloyd was managing editor for *Teen Life* magazine, and has tutored at the Borough of Manhattan Community College's Writing Center. She lives in New York City and counsels students at Baruch College. Mrs. Lloyd has published one novel, and is currently at work on another.

Arthur M. Schlesinger, jr., taught history at Harvard for many years and is currently Albert Schweitzer Professor of the Humanities at City University of New York. He is the author of numerous highly praised works in American history and has twice been awarded the Pulitzer Prize. He served in the White House as special assistant to Presidents Kennedy and Johnson.